P9-CDE-474

THE LANGUAGE OF ORDINATION

Ministry in an Ecumenical Context

L. William Countryman

Trinity Press International
Philadelphia

First Published 1992

Trinity Press International
3725 Chestnut Street
Philadelphia, PA 19104

All rights reserved. No part of this publication may be reproduced, stored in a retrieval system, or transmitted, in any form or by any means, electronic, mechanical, photocopying, recording or otherwise, without the prior permission of the publisher, Trinity Press International.

© 1992 L. William Countryman

Cover design by Jim Gerhard

Countryman, Louis William, 1941–
    The language of ordination : ministry in an ecumenical context /
L. William Countryman.
        p.   cm.
    Includes bibliographical references.
    ISBN 1-56338-046-3 (pbk.)
    1. Ordination.   2. Ecumenical movement.   I. Title
BV664.5.C68   1992
262'.1—dc20   92-21970
                                                                   CIP

Printed in the United States of America

Contents

Preface

I OWE A DEBT TO MANY PEOPLE WHO HAVE BEEN PARTNERS IN dialogue about ministry and ordination over the past three decades. I could not begin to name and thank them all. With regard to the present work, however, I am particularly indebted to two friends and colleagues who read the manuscript for me, Shunji Nishi and Michael Wyatt, and to Hal Rast of Trinity Press International. Their helpful and critical comments have occasioned much improvement in the work. Eight years of experience in Lutheran-Episcopal Dialogue, Series III, have helped me to refine and clarify the ideas found here, though their origins go back much further in my own thinking.

As the relative paucity of footnotes will suggest, this is a work of theological reflection more than of academic scholarship. I have not brought forward any new data nor attempted to offer a summary of the current state of the discussion, but only offered a certain way of looking at the issues posed by holy orders. I hope that this particular perspective might suggest a way in which Christians can both esteem the variety that has characterized our past and also move toward greater unity in our future. For historical data, I have deliberately referred to basic, commonly available works, rather than to more arcane scholarship, preferring to work with the present consensus rather than try to construct anything new. Biblical quotations are my own translations.

Introduction

MINISTRY AND ORDINATION HAVE BECOME DIFFICULT TOPICS FOR
the church in the present generation. It once seemed clear that the
ordained are ministers and the unordained, "the laity," are not. It
seemed clear that ministers received a special divine call over and
above their baptism. In most churches, it was clear that they
needed extensive educational preparation as well. It seemed clear
that the ordained were a special—probably a superior—category
of Christian. And it seemed clear to each individual denomination
that its own way of structuring and defining the ordained ministry was the ideal, compared with the ways of other church traditions which were clearly inferior.

In the last decade of the twentieth century, even though there
are as yet few clear alternatives to this kind of thinking, none of
these certainties is any longer beyond question. A renewed appreciation of baptism has undermined theories of ministry that,
overtly or covertly, turned the ordained into a superior class of
Christians—theories that threatened to make ordination a more
important sacrament than baptism itself. A question mark has
thus been set next to ordination in the life of individual church
traditions.

At the same time, ordination has proven to be a major sticking
point in efforts to draw diverse traditions of Christians together
in the creation of a more ecumenical future for the churches.
Anglicans may be more conscious of this fact than most, since we
are often the ones stuck in the middle—and also the ones blamed
for the fact that ordination is a sticking point at all. Still, the
problem is there. Reunion even between closely related denominations is difficult. Between truly diverse traditions within Christianity, it is still practically unknown in the West, despite certain

1

successes in Asia. The problem of orders is one important part of the complex of issues that has made change slow to come.

We have, then, two sets of problems: How are the ordained related to those not ordained? How do different traditions of orders relate to one another? The two questions are related in important ways, but they are of concern to somewhat different groups of people. I hope to explore the larger issues more fully in another work, dealing with the priesthood of the whole people of God and that of the ordained and how they are interrelated. The present study, however, will focus on the ecumenical issue: how we can understand ordination in such a way that we do some justice to the values our various denominations have placed on it in the past and also leave ourselves open to a future in which our orders may help initiate a renewal of Christian unity.

Perhaps this is an impossible task. Certainly it seems to contain a conundrum. I want to appreciate and honor our existing traditions, built on the foundation and refined in the context of Christian division, and I also to make an opening toward a future that includes motion toward rather than away from unity. What is more, I am doing this at a time when traumatic disputes about the Christian message and its understanding in the modern world make new divisions seem more likely than enhanced unity. There is no other way, however, to go about the task than to insist on trying to hold past and future together—everybody's past and everybody's future. And if we wait for ideal circumstances in order to think theologically and ecumenically, we may be waiting a very long time indeed.

There is no point in discussing orders at all without emphasizing how deeply embedded they are in tradition, the historical and ongoing life of each different Christian community. Theology alone will never give us an accurate assessment of what orders really mean for anyone. Even in churches that appear theologically and liturgically similar in this regard, the similarities often mask far-reaching differences. Anglicans and Roman Catholics, for example, have very similar rites of ordination.[1] Each tradition believes that their bishops stand in some kind of historic succession reaching back to the earliest Christians. They agree in recognizing three orders to which a person is separately ordained: bishop, priest (or presbyter), and deacon. Yet the meaning of all this for the average American Roman Catholic or Episcopalian is likely to be quite different. Where an Episcopal bishop is elected by the diocese and confirmed by other Episcopal dioceses, a Roman bishop is appointed by Rome from a short list of nominees made by other American bishops. Where an Episcopal bishop's authority is fairly modest, that of a Roman bishop is much more extensive. Where an Episcopal bishop bears heavy responsibility for formulating the official teaching of the Episcopal Church, functioning as member of a house of bishops that is fairly open about its internal disagreements and that has no authority above it that can override its decisions, a Roman bishop is seen primarily as spokesman for a relatively uniform denomination whose policies are centrally determined. The Episcopal bishop would be unintelligible in a Roman Catholic context; the Roman bishop would be at a loss as to how to function in an Episcopal context.

The specific life of each denomination, then, varies greatly in its use of the ordained and in the functions ascribed to them. In comparison, the mere similarity of ordination rites might seem insignificant. That is, however, far from being true. Despite the significant differences between the two, both Anglicans and Roman Catholics have the (sometimes uneasy) sense that their bishops belong to the same category, and this sense is based on the similarity of their *orders*—of the way in which they are ordained and the networks of ordination to which they belong. Without this sense of relatedness, Romans and Anglicans would have spilled no ink in efforts to disprove or prove their equivalence. The particulars of ordination itself, seemingly inconsequential in comparison to the daily realities of episcopal functioning, have an uncanny power to shape our sense of ecclesial reality.

Christians share a common concern—sometimes relatively inarticulate—with orders; yet orders are bound up with the communal identities that particularly divide us from one another here and now. The challenge is how to take our diversity of traditions seriously and, at the same time, keep them alive and open and pointed toward an ecumenical future. In and of themselves, our varying traditions tend only to repeat the past and compose variations on it. Unless they can learn to do something new, they cannot move toward ecumenical unity. Anglicans can go on refuting Romanism and Puritanism. Methodists can go on calling for a heartwarming alternative to eighteenth-century head religion. Disciples of Christ can keep practicing early nineteenth-century primitivism. Lutherans can continue to guard their doctrinal purity and Roman Catholics their dogmatic priority until the world grows cold. It will never lead to any sort of unity—only to improved insulation between our separate tracks.

There will be no progress unless we take our traditions with utmost seriousness, and no progress unless we also do more. Our theological righteousness will have to exceed that of the polemicists of prior centuries who dug the hardened bunkers in which we are now living. By that I mean not that we must forget their work, but that we must do it better and with a broader and more adequate purpose in mind. We cannot turn out backs on our denominational traditions. They tell us who we are as Christian communities. We must take them seriously, live within them, and develop them—but this time with an idea to making windows instead of gunports. All of this means for me that I am writing something that is self-consciously Anglican at the same time that it is self-consciously ecumenical. I do not possess the insight to write from a Methodist, a Lutheran, a Roman, a Russian Orthodox, a Quaker, or a Presbyterian perspective. I hope, however, to draw on Anglican tradition in this matter of orders to suggest a way of analyzing and talking about the problems—a way that all of us might be able to use to begin constructing a viewpoint on the matter that could unite rather than further divide.

The past is basic to adult human identity. All of us may have some areas of selective amnesia; but, on the whole, we think of the victims of amnesia as unfortunate because they have lost massive parts of who they are. Still, the past is never a full or sufficient definition of a person, that is, until the person is dead. Sometimes taking the next step in our lives demands turning our backs on some aspect of our past or, at the very least, recognizing the ways in which our past hinders us and choosing to build on some parts of it rather than others. There are at least two elements in the history of orders that present exactly such barriers for us. We shall have to learn how to build on the past in a way that relativizes and restricts their influence. While I will be dealing with these in some sense throughout what follows, I should like to highlight them here at the beginning.

The first of these problematic elements is a quality inherent in the classic model of orders beloved of Anglicans. This model was originally devised in large part to discourage schism; it focused the identity of the local church strongly in a single person, the bishop, so that it would be difficult for any person or group splitting off from the community to claim continuity with the original church. It was created in reaction against the fissiparous tendencies that plagued Christianity from its earliest days (and plague it still). It was well designed for this purpose and therefore not well designed for the ecumenical purpose—the purpose of repairing splits in the church that are now, in most cases, centuries old. This does not mean that the classic model of orders is useless, but it does mean that those of us who care about it must recognize its limitations and ask how the church can respectfully transcend them.

The other great historical barrier that we face in the West dates from the era of the Reformation and thereafter. Until that time, the basic pattern of orders was broadly consistent over space and time; since then, it has become fragmented. That, however, is not the worst of the problem. The worst is that ordination was used on all sides during the Reformation and in subsequent intra-Protestant divisions as a way of making distinctions among emerging groups. The Reformed tradition, for example, did not merely revise the existing pattern of orders but began to claim that their revised pattern was the only one divinely and scripturally authorized. Apologetic on behalf of Reformed practices shaded off easily enough into criticism of others and outright polemic. Advocates of other patterns responded in kind. Orders quickly became a major point not merely of difference but of contention.

In the modern situation, then, the churches inherit a classic pattern of orders originally designed to prevent division in the church rather than to heal it, and also a Reformation and post-Reformation penchant for using our differences about orders as a stick with which to beat one another. A nasty situation indeed. And Anglicans have been more or less in the middle of it, though perhaps more by accident/providence than by intention. If Anglicans have anything in particular to contribute to the resolution of the problems, I think it arises from the awkwardness of out historic situation. We are, as the saying goes, both Catholic and Protestant. That does not make us a blend of the two or an intermediate stage, still less (despite our own wishful thinking) a bridge. (Or, if we are a bridge, we seem to be one that nobody much wants to cross even if they would like to get to the other side!) It does, however, give us a unique perspective, one from which a person might hope at least to appreciate the problems at both ends of the bridge—the problem with the classical pattern of orders and the problem with the polemicized multiplicity of patterns that emerged from the Reformation.

As an Anglican writing for ecumenical reasons, I hope to offer here not a formula that would take us around the current impasse, but a way of thinking and talking about orders that could conceivably bring our diverse traditions into a single universe of discourse that is not identical with any one of them. I hope to propose a way of thinking of orders—and, eventually, doing something about them—that can honor our separate traditions while also freeing them to grow toward one another rather than away. My proposal, in brief, is that we should understand orders (by which I mean especially the social and physical acts of ordination itself) as a way in which Christian communities create tangible, personal sacraments of their life under the gospel. We may even think of orders as a kind of language in which such communities define or describe themselves both to their own members and to one another. Different ways of structuring orders (presbyterian, for example, as opposed to episcopalian) will then prove to be different "sentences" spoken in the same language. This does not imply that the differences are therefore negligible; it is rare that the difference between any two sentences in the same language is negligible. But it will give us a way to compare our diversities that does not rush immediately to label them "right" or "wrong." Instead, we shall have the opportunity to find out whether there is in fact some common sentence that we really wish to utter together about being Christian, about being communities—or the community—of the good news.

As I endeavor to lay this argument out, you, my readers, are a problem. I expect that you are a very diverse audience with diverse presuppositions. In the classroom, as a teacher of New Testament, I am sometimes confronted with a class that includes some people who are quasi-fundamentalist in their presuppositions about scripture, some who dismiss biblical authority altogether, and a good many who are in-between. It is difficult—perhaps impossible—to speak to all of their concerns at once. Similarly, the ecumenical audience includes a great range of presuppositions. There are people for whom orders are presumed as a fixed and nonproblematic issue; or if there is a problem, it is only the problem of persuading others to see and accept "our" solution. It also includes people who believe that orders are of no importance at all, or believe that they believe this until someone suggests certain alterations in their own way of doing things. It includes those who see orders as a peripheral problem best dealt with by marginalizing it, and also those who see orders as a central issue and critical to further progress. Probably no one book can hope to address all of these perspectives, but I think this book does have consequences for all of them.

To Anglicans (and, by implication, to other Christians who maintain the historic episcopate), I hope to show that we can do theological justice to our ecclesial experience and the tradition that sustains it without resorting to triumphalism. We can argue for the historic episcopate as a good without having to imply that the historical alternatives in use among other denominations are evils. To those Christians less friendly toward the historic episcopate, I hope to show that its value is general and ecumenical, not merely denominational or historically contingent. To all alike, Catholic and Protestant, I hope to show that there are terms in which we can be mutually appreciative and affirming of one another's orders, working together to preserve what is positive in our traditions, to let go of polemical elements in them, and to renew these traditions in ways leading to a more ecumenical future.

Chapter 1

Orders as Ecumenical Problem

THE HISTORIC EPISCOPATE AND
ANGLICAN ECUMENICAL EXPERIENCE

I BEGIN, AS I MUST, FROM AN ANGLICAN STARTING POINT. ORDERS have long been a key issue for Anglicans in ecumenical discussion. This is implicit, for example, in the fourth point of the Chicago-Lambeth Quadrilateral, which has been the foundation of modern Anglican ecumenical endeavors. The Quadrilateral is worth quoting to illustrate the high evaluation Anglicans place on a certain way of ordaining.

The following Articles supply a basis on which approach may be by God's blessing made towards . . . Reunion:

(a) The Holy Scriptures of the Old and New Testaments, as "containing all things necessary to salvation," and as being the rule and ultimate standard of faith.

(b) The Apostles' Creed, as the Baptismal Symbol; and the Nicene Creed, as the sufficient statement of the Christian faith.

(c) The two Sacraments ordained by Christ Himself—Baptism and the Supper of the Lord—ministered with unfailing use of Christ's words of Institution, and of the elements ordained by Him.

(d) The Historic Episcopate, locally adapted in the methods of its administration to the varying needs of the nations and peoples called of God into the Unity of His Church.[1]

The Quadrilateral places a certain description of orders (the "Historic Episcopate") alongside the other most nearly unquestionable institutions of Christianity: scripture, the two principal sacraments, and the two ancient creeds. In doing so, it represents substantive and longstanding Anglican sentiment. It is not one of those innumerable ecclesiastical pronouncements forgotten the day after it was issued. To the contrary, it succeeded in formulating a significant aspect of our elusive Anglican ethos; and, as a result, it has become a constant reference point for Anglican perspective on ecumenical issues. Anglicans have no single, common, official explanation of *why* the historic episcopate is important; but we overwhelmingly concur in the consensus that it is.

A brief glance over modern Anglican ecumenical history, however, shows that the question of orders has been a difficulty more often than a help in bringing Christians together.[2] To be sure, there have been a few cases where it has not been a question at all, since each side could agree that the historic episcopate was present in the other's tradition. This was the case, for example, in relation to Old Catholics in communion with Utrecht and with the Church of Sweden. In a few other cases, churches that lacked the historic episcopate because of accidents of history were happy to reclaim it in the process of entering into full communion with Anglicans. Such was the story of the Philippine Independent Church.

These relatively simple situations, however, are the exceptions and not the rule. Outside the Anglican tradition, most churches reshaped by the Reformation—and most of those originating since then—either rejected episcopacy as such or else broke the historic succession of episcopal ordinations. To some of them, resumption of the historic episcopate seems a denial of their own principles. To others, it seems an irrelevance or even an affectation. In Great Britain, the United States, and elsewhere, a number of schemes for Anglican reunion with such churches have at least stumbled over the problems of episcopacy and ordination—some because other Protestants felt that Anglicans demanded too much, others because some Anglicans felt that too much had been compromised.

Even apart from the reunion schemes that have failed outright, some of those that have gone forward get mixed responses from the worldwide Anglican communion. The Church of South India, for example, committed itself from the start to the full unification of its ministry within the framework of the historic episcopate.

Yet other Anglican churches had reservations about the interim period before the new church's ministry was completely unified. Until the process was completed, nonepiscopally ordained clergy continued to function alongside those episcopally ordained, with the same status and authority. Even now, the Church of South India continues to receive overseas clergy from all the traditions that gave it birth and allows them to function without being reordained. And even now, the Church of South India is perhaps less than fully accepted by other Anglicans.

The unions that created the Churches of North India and Pakistan sought to avoid these problems by unifying the ministries from the beginning. They used a freshly constructed rite that included laying on of hands, but was not specific about what was being accomplished thereby. While this received better acceptance and has inspired some subsequent proposals in other parts of the world, it is still an uncomfortable solution for many precisely because of its vague and indeterminate quality. It appears to be a decision not to decide on the issues.

Such a decision may be acceptable if it contributes to the realization of Christian love. It implies, however, that the issue of ordination is purely a barrier to be gotten over, not anything that might contribute to our understanding of the gospel or of the meaning of the church. As such, it fails to do justice to the Chicago-Lambeth Quadrilateral, which offered the historic episcopate as a mainstay of ecumenism. While Anglicans, being happily free of any tradition of ecclesiastical infallibility, are not bound forever to that statement, we cannot appropriately abandon it without, at least, some serious and deliberate reflection.

The problems I have just mentioned exist on the Protestant side of our ecumenical relationships. Another set of problems appears on the Catholic side. The Eastern Orthodox appear unwilling to separate the issue of the historic episcopate from other aspects of tradition. Roman Catholics, on the other hand, share with us a rough, general agreement about the nature and importance of the historic episcopate, but deny that it is found among Anglicans. In neither case can the Anglican Church do much to affect the situation directly. Still, becoming clear about our own understanding of the issues is essential to further dialogue.

Three sets of problems thus emerge across the broad spectrum of Anglican ecumenical experience. First, there is the problem that most Protestant churches have with our insistence on the historic episcopate. Second, there is lack of agreement about the precise meaning of the historic episcopate within Anglicanism itself so that some Anglicans may object to solutions that other Anglicans find satisfactory. (The same lack of agreement is also causing pain within Anglicanism over the ordination of women to the presbyterate and episcopate.) Third, there is the range of problems felt by most of our Catholic coreligionists who are reluctant to acknowledge that the historic episcopate actually exists in the Anglican churches.

In a sense, we Anglicans find ourselves, vis-à-vis the Church of Rome, in roughly the same position that most of our Protestant sisters and brothers are in vis-à-vis us. In each case, the more "Catholic" group is saying to the more "Protestant" group that something more is required for unity—a something more that perhaps could cast doubt on the ecclesiastical integrity of the more "Protestant" body's past and present. It may be helpful, then, not only to our dialogues with Protestants but to the ecumenical situation at large if Anglicans can understand what Protestants find objectionable about our insistence on the historic episcopate. Why is it a stumbling block for those of our coreligionists who do not share in it?

The central objection is that Anglican insistence on the historic episcopate has the effect of adding something to the gospel itself as a condition of unity. The other elements of the Chicago-Lambeth Quadrilateral are less problematic. Very few Protestants have any difficulty about the Holy Scriptures or the two dominical sacraments as foundations for church unity. Some, such as the Disciples of Christ, do have difficulty with creeds, but often less with their substance than with a fear that they may be used in a legalistic manner to forestall open and honest exploration of the faith. All of these things—scripture, sacraments, creeds—can be understood as means by which the gospel is communicated. Without them, we would all have difficulty articulating what the gospel is. They are pretty readily accepted as basic.

The historic episcopate, however, may seem to be more about the church than about the gospel—and not even about the church as a whole, but about the prideful claims of certain fragments of the church to be purer and more pleasing to God than other fragments thereof. Surely, some would argue, Anglicans have here left the foundations of the gospel with its message of gracious forgiveness and free redemption and taken a stand, instead, on ecclesiastical works. Since Anglicans insist that certain rites be performed in a certain way, we appear to have made the salvation of humanity (or, at least, the constitution of the church) dependent on the correct execution of certain ceremonies.

At the extreme, Anglican insistence on the historic episcopate might appear to unchurch many other Christians, suggesting that their communities are so defective constitutionally that they do not qualify as loci where the salvation offered by God to all people becomes available. In fact, there have been Anglicans, mostly of the high-church tradition, who have said something very much like that. While not necessarily trying to limit God's grace in general, they have held that, as a rule, only the historic episcopate can be counted on to mediate it. Even though this is neither a majority belief in Anglicanism nor an official one, it necessarily colors others' perception of our tradition. In ecumenical conversation, Anglicans have tried to overcome this impression of what we mean by a respectful attitude toward the communities and ministries of our brothers and sisters in Protestant communions. Still, the suspicion remains and is not entirely without plausibility.

Even where Anglicans have already made it clear that we see in a nonepiscopal church a true community of the faithful with an effective ministry, it remains true that, for the future, Anglicans do want that church to adopt the pattern of orders we call "historic episcopate." The Episcopal Church, for example, has entered into "Interim Eucharistic Sharing" with the Evangelical Lutheran Church in America. This arrangement surely implies recognition of the genuineness of ministry and sacraments in a church without what we call the "historic episcopate." Yet recent efforts to move toward full communion between the two churches seem, at this writing, to be foundering on the reef of differences over orders.

Some Lutherans apparently feel that Anglicans are laying on them a burden comparable to the burden of circumcision, which many early Christians wished to lay on Gentile converts. To them, we still seem to be saying, "If you want to be a *real* church, you must do it our way."

A NEW "CIRCUMCISION" CONTROVERSY?

In the circumcision controversy, two very different views about the gospel came into conflict. The more liberal view of the Hellenists and Paul said that the gospel was absolutely free to all, without prior conditions. A Gentile could therefore respond to the gospel with faith and still continue to be in all respects a Gentile; if there were restrictions on Gentile behavior, from this perspective they were only those that were minimally necessary in order to preserve mutual respect and communion between Jewish and Gentile Christians. The view of the circumcision party, however, was that while God's grace was free to all, a Gentile convert must become in some sense Jewish (through circumcision, in the case of a male) in order to claim it. Grace, it seems, was free, but at a price.

While the original circumcision controversy was settled in favor of the liberals (Paul and the Hellenists), the conflict of principles behind it has never ceased to devil Christians; and the heirs of the circumcision party have often been the winners in subsequent conflicts. This is perhaps most obvious to the contemporary observer in the context of modern Christian missions, where the gospel preached has often looked and sounded suspiciously like a pious version of European or American culture, and where conversion has often meant abandoning indigenous culture or even execrating it. Gentiles of European or Euro-American extraction have often failed to extend to others the courtesy—not to mention the freedom of the gospel—shown our forebears in the first century.

In a similar vein, it appears to some that the Anglican case for adoption of the historic episcopate is a kind of cultural price tag attached to the gospel. Even if Anglicans are ready to acknowledge the effectiveness of nonepiscopal ministries within existing

Protestant churches, we may seem to imply that something more is demanded if Protestants would be part of the "true" church, the true arena of God's grace. It appears to be another chapter in the long Christian saga of "We want you among us, but not as you are—only if you will become like us, the people truly acceptable to God."

These are grave charges, particularly when leveled against a church that has historically renounced the idea of "works of supererogation" (Article XIV) and called the principle of justification by faith "a most wholesome Doctrine" (Article XI).[3] What is worse, it is difficult to deny that these charges have some basis in fact. Anglicans have behaved variously toward ministers of other Protestant denominations under varying circumstances, but with a tendency, over the last three centuries or so, to look down on or exclude ministries different from our own.

There was a time when the Church of England, even though it treated homegrown dissenters negatively, accepted the occasional visiting Protestant minister from the Continent without substantial qualms. After 1662, however, no one could function as an ordained person in Anglicanism without episcopal ordination.[4] In America, these distinctions would have been hard to maintain in any case, since it was seldom entirely clear who was a dissenter from the Church of England and who came from an independent tradition such as that of the Netherlands or Sweden. The result was a tendency to think simply of Anglicans and "others." In the nineteenth century, with the Oxford Movement, there was an increasing tendency to focus on the historic episcopate (often called "apostolic succession") as the principal justification for Anglicanism's very existence, with a corresponding tendency to downgrade all other forms of ministry and ordination or even to discount them altogether.

One common way of stating this was to question the "validity" of other ministries, often specifically in relation to the question of whether they had the right, authority, or power to preside at the eucharist or to convey the absolution of sins. Nonepiscopal ministries were held to be either invalid or, in an effort to make the condemnation sound less sweeping, "defective." At the extreme, some Anglicans held to a "pipeline" theory of ordination.

The original apostles, according to this theory, were given power to bestow blessings and perform sacraments (specifically the eucharist, absolution, confirmation, anointing, and ordination).[5] They passed these on, through laying on of hands, to their successors, and they to their successors, and so on down to the present bishop of the local diocese and, in lesser degree, to the priest of the local parish, whose correct and apostolic ordination rendered the parish eucharist "valid." Properly ordained clergy thus formed the plumbing through which the waters of grace flowed, emerging at the spigots of the sacraments.

Needless to say, the most excellent plumbing in the world, if it was not connected to its source, would convey nothing whatever. This, it was to be feared, was the case with most Protestant ministries. God, to be sure, would not forsake faithful people and might very well distribute "uncovenanted" grace to people outside the system of correct ordinations, perhaps even using other ministries in the process. But only the historic episcopate came, as it were, with a guarantee.

At no time was this ever an official teaching of Anglicanism, but it was widespread in some areas and in certain schools of thought. Consequently, it has left behind it a lingering suspicion on the part of non-Anglicans that our apparent intransigence in insisting on the historic episcopate is a more covert form of the same teaching. Modern decay of the pipeline theory may pave the way for disappearance of this anxiety among our Protestant sisters and brothers. There are signs of this already, most notably the "Lima document" of Faith and Order entitled *Baptism, Eucharist and Ministry.*[6] In it, a broadly ecumenical gathering produced a call for all churches to recover and renew the historic episcopate in the process of moving toward future realization of Christian unity. There is no certainty, however, that churches will follow the lead of Lima; and the perception that Anglicans are still secretly committed to a pipeline theory will be a barrier to such movement for Protestants generally.

It should not be difficult for Anglicans to sympathize with this objection. Most of us would be quite unwilling to accept reordination of our clergy as part of the price of unity with the Roman Church. We would reject any implication that somehow

the ministrations that have characterized our church life were not
"real," or were less "real" than those of some other Christian
body. Even if we can make it quite clear that restoration of the
historic episcopate is not intended to imply any lack of validity in
the existing ministries of other churches, it might still seem like a
rite of circumcision demanded of the Gentiles, reminding them
that they were not really quite good enough for God or for us as
they were.

PURITY

Today circumcision is essentially a purity rite. I have argued elsewhere that that is precisely why the earliest Christians could not
allow it to become a requirement for admission into the Christian
community.[7] Similar concerns with purity are sometimes at work
in our discussions of ordination—not surprisingly—since ordination involves touch, and touch is potentially a source of impurity.
While this is not the place for a detailed discussion of the topic, a
few general remarks about purity will prove helpful for subsequent
discussion of the problems surrounding orders. Purity rules are
rules distinguishing between what is "pure" or "clean" and what is
"impure, unclean, dirty." They apply particularly to the human
body and the things that touch or enter or leave it. They often
overlap with other kinds of ethical and religious concerns, but are
not identical with them. Purity is unlike other ethical concerns, for
example, in that human intention is not a major factor. It makes no
difference whether you *meant* to come into contact with something
unclean; if you did, you are now unclean yourself.

Concern for purity is a widespread human phenomenon. All cultures seem to have purity codes, though they vary greatly in their
complexity and in how seriously they are taken. In the tradition of
Israel and often in later Christianity, purity has been intimately
associated with holiness and therefore with access to God. Only the
pure could approach the Temple and participate in the sacrifices. As
inhabitants of the Temple, priests had to be the purest Israelites of
all. No wonder early Jewish Christians felt that it was inappropriate
for the uncircumcised to be baptized and participate in their sacred
meal. Not only was the lack of circumcision inherently unclean,

according to their inherited and scriptural purity code, it was part and parcel of an entire culture that, from their perspective, was ignorant of real purity and indifferent to it.

The problem, however, touched them more nearly than that. If the baptism of the uncircumcised had merely seemed inappropriate, the circumcision party might have adapted to it as something undesirable but endurable for the sake of Christian unity. For them, however, it was not merely inappropriate; it was directly threatening. One constant presupposition of the Israelite purity codes is that impurity is easier to contract than to get rid of. All you need do is eat a forbidden food—or one treated in the wrong manner—or be touched by a menstruating woman or find yourself under the same roof with a corpse. You are rendered unclean and therefore unsuitable to approach God. How could anyone committed to staying pure and living in God's presence eat the sacred meal of the church with equanimity—seated next to a Gentile, a person whose very presence radiated filth?

When taken with great seriousness, purity codes require a defensive mode of living. Unfortunately, they also encourage some vicious behavior that was probably far from the intentions of their originators. They encourage efforts to segregate the unclean, who usually also turn out to be people of relatively low social standing. They encourage the clean to identify their purity with godliness and therefore to assume that God smiles on them and on them alone. Purity rules easily become the prime example and supreme opportunity for a religion of works-righteousness. They are simple, unambiguous, and quantifiable. They make it easy to estimate my position in God's eyes and the eyes of the community relative to yours. They tempt me, like the obedient brother in the parable of the Prodigal Son or the Pharisee at prayer in the Temple, to think of myself as having earned God's good opinion. They almost compel me to construct a world of insiders and outsiders—one in which I am insider, of course, and you are outsider. This does not make purity codes intrinsically wrong, but it does make them very hard to reconcile with a world of grace in which everything exists and is redeemed by God's gift and not by our own deserving.

This is no doubt the reason why Jesus bracketed the purity codes of Israel, both oral and written. He did not forbid anyone to observe them, but he separated purity sharply from access to God. In place of literal purity (what we sometimes call "ritual" purity, but what we might better think of as "physical" purity), he substituted "purity of the heart." It is not what enters into you from without, he said, that can make you impure, but what comes out of your heart—in ancient Mediterranean language, the organ of thinking and planning more than of feeling (Mark 7:14–23). When you try to harm your neighbor, *that* makes you unclean and unfit to approach God. Eating unclean food, menstruating, being a leper, touching a corpse—these do not exclude you from access to God.

Paul was following Jesus' lead, then, when he insisted that purity rules were fundamentally irrelevant for Christians and that lack of circumcision was no barrier to membership in the church. He encouraged the "strong," who were relatively indifferent to purity, not to provoke the "weak," who took it more seriously. He allowed that, if your own conscience required you to keep purity, you ought to do so, though you must not become judgmental in relation to the "strong." What he could not and would not allow under any circumstances was that you had to be pure in the literal, physical sense in order to approach God or to be a full member of the Christian community.[8]

Ordained ministry has a regrettable but natural affinity for purity rules. It forms a natural arena for them. The ordained wash us in baptism, handle our food in the eucharist, preside at weddings and funerals. Moreover, ordination itself involves touching, the same kind of touching that can convey the contagions of impurity as well. I shall say more about this topic in a subsequent chapter, but it is useful to raise it here because of the way it can illuminate ordination as an ecumenical problem. Much of the anxiety all of us feel about any possibility of change in ordination practices has to do with precisely these fundamental, primeval human fears about contamination. If we allow any change in the way orders are administered, we fear that God will be less pleased and less accessible as a result.

This is true on all sides of the problem. Anglicans are afraid
that our ministry will be contaminated (or, at least, diluted) if it is
merged with others and that God will be less pleased with us. But
Lutherans, Roman Catholics, Presbyterians, and others are at least
equally afraid—afraid of what is foreign, alien, unclean to them.
It is said that there is one Protestant state church on the continent
of Europe that always invites bishops from a neighboring state
church (belonging to the same Reformation tradition) to the ordination of its bishops and then stations a seminarian to make sure
that the foreign bishops do not touch the ordinand at the laying on
of hands. For the new bishop would then be impure and would
contract contagion of the kind most deeply feared by human beings—not the contagion of germs (a relatively modern notion, in
any case), but the contagion of impurity, of foreignness, of an
alien succession, of something that might be less pleasing to God
than one's own tradition. It is a chance no one would take lightly,
least of all the pious.

Only in the gospel, which declares that grace is given freely to
all, clean and unclean alike, is it possible for pious people to take
such a chance. Yet in the gospel, it is *possible*. The question that
follows is whether it is also *desirable*. The answer will turn on
whether we see ourselves as standing to gain something of value by
taking this risk. With regard to the historic episcopate, the risk
can be worthwhile only if it offers something more than simply
the defining of one community against another or a bid for favor
with God. To be worthwhile, the historic episcopate must—like
scriptures, sacraments, creeds—embody something of the gospel
itself that Christians would want to unite in preserving and propa-
gating. Even then, our joining together must take place without
any falsification or denial of the past, with all of its difficulties,
blessings, and failures on all sides.

Implicit in all I have said up to now is that ministry and church
identity are very intimately mixed up together not only for Anglicans but for Christians of all sorts. As a result, it is difficult to
make any substantive changes in ordination without appearing to
challenge the continuity of the community involved—without,
for that matter, appearing to condemn and demolish the past and
establish a new order on its ruins. Fears for the purity of the

ministry combine with a natural desire to preserve the identity of one's community. Together, these considerations make change very difficult.

If Anglicans wish to urge the historic episcopate on others in the process of ecumenical convergence, we must be clear that we are not suggesting a negative evaluation of other traditions or claiming that one must be Anglicanized before one can be pleasing to God. We require an explanation of the historic episcopate continuous with our own tradition and experience, while also showing that it has a valuable contribution to make for the proclamation of the gospel in the ecumenical church of the future. If we cannot find ways to make this case without resorting to claims, explicit or implicit, that we are uniquely pure and pleasing to God or that we alone enjoy real grace or that others must be transformed and become like us, then we cannot expect to make the case at all. For it would be a different case then, not a claim on behalf of the gospel but one on behalf of our own purity and merit. It will rightly be ignored, and we shall need to think again whether we as people of the gospel wish to make such a claim at all.

Chapter 2

Some Basic Presuppositions

It has become a truism of recent thought that there is no such thing as objectivity. While I am less skeptical on this matter than many of my academic colleagues, in the present instance I have no wish to claim objectivity (except in the limited sense that I shall try to think, and to present my thinking, as clearly as possible and in a way that can be tested and criticized by others). Instead, I wish to claim the specific perspective of an Anglican who has a strong concern for and some experience in ecumenics. I seek to remain rooted in a specific Christian tradition while also endeavoring to look outward to a larger world and to a future that I hope will be less fragmented than our past and present.

Accordingly, I want to be specific about the values that form the foundation of my inquiry here. Probably one can never be perfectly conscious of or explicit about one's own presuppositions. I think, however, that even partial success will be pertinent to this argument and will help clarify what follows. There are three main points I want to affirm: (1) The gospel is primary. (2) Ordained ministry is a sacrament of the church's life. (3) The four classic "notes" of the church must therefore be manifest in the church's ministry.

THE GOSPEL IS PRIMARY

I consider the ordained ministry an important but not a fundamental issue for Christians. The fundamental issue is and must always be the gospel. By "the gospel" I mean quite specifically Jesus' good news of free forgiveness. Our standing before God is no longer based on our own goodness, but purely and simply on God's gift to us of grace. As Christians, we know this grace as forgiveness—even for sins we have not yet recognized or repented of—and also as life, love, understanding, joy, and all of the good things that we share with the rest of humanity. None of these comes ultimately from us; all is from God—often, however, through the agency of other people.

We are told to respond to learning of God's gifts with love for God and for one another. Neither of these is an arbitrary demand. Love for the giver is the only way to acknowledge reception of the gift. And once we acknowledge the gift and see that our whole standing before God is entirely the result of God's gift, we begin to understand that our neighbor is in exactly the same situation as we are. With God there is no partiality, no respect of persons, no greater or lesser. Therefore, as one gifted with grace, I cannot make a distinction between my own deserving and that of my neighbor. We both are in exactly the same position before God. I shall therefore begin to learn to love self and neighbor equally, because we are, in fact, equals.

If we no longer have this good news to tell people (ourselves included), we are no longer followers of Jesus, whatever label we may bear. Conversely, Jesus himself was quite prepared to claim kinship with anyone who brought good news, even if that person was not a part of his following.[1] The good news is fundamental in a way that nothing else in Christian tradition can ever be. If at any point circumstances should force us to choose between faithfulness to the gospel and faithfulness to any other aspect of the tradition—church, ordained ministry, doctrinal definitions, or whatever—the only authentically Christian choice is to prefer the gospel over everything else.

In the normal course of events, we should not be in a hurry to suppose that we have to make such either-or decisions. While the Christian community is never perfect, either as a whole or in its various separate streams, it is still the principal means by which the good news is preserved and proclaimed. To accept a certain level of imperfection in ourselves and in our communities is to acknowledge the truth that we are all finite, developing human beings. To demand perfection would be to pretend that the church is a kind of angelic or even divine reality without human weaknesses. Whatever Christians may mean by professing belief in "one, holy, catholic, and apostolic church," it can scarcely be the same thing we mean by confessing belief in God. We have no reason in the gospel to confuse the church with God, and any such confusion will inevitably redound to the discrediting of our message and to sinful excesses on the part of the church.

The church, then, is a kind of secondary manifestation of things Christian. It emerges from the gospel as a community of those who have heard the good news of forgiveness and received it; and it takes up the challenge of sharing the good news with others. In doing so, it develops an array of institutional forms designed to enable the carrying of the message across boundaries of time and space—from generation to generation and from one human community (as defined by geography, ethnicity, class, culture, or whatever) to another.

As with all ongoing institutions, the church tends to think of itself as its own reason for being. When it does, it begins to fail in its task. One virtue of the church's institutional structure, however, is that it includes elements designed to remind the church of its real reason for existence. I have argued elsewhere that this is the central reason why we have a canon of scriptures in Christianity.[2] When the church becomes mired in self-absorption and the myopia of the present moment, the scriptures witness to more important things. The great sacraments of baptism and eucharist also fulfill this function by focusing our attention on the absolute priority of God's grace—what God does for us rather than what we do for God. The creeds do something similar by emphasizing the life, death, and resurrection of Jesus and connecting these with creation, on the one hand, and the ongoing work of the Spirit, on the other. If the ordained ministry is, as the Chicago-Lambeth Quadrilateral suggests, comparable to scriptures, sacrament, and creeds, it ought to have some similar role to play.

One might describe the ordained ministry as a kind of tertiary reality of Christian faith, derivative from the Christian community as the community itself is from the gospel. And yet, though not entirely untrue, that is perhaps a misleading way to state the matter. For it implies that the church, at some point, existed without any structure at all. That is hardly conceivable. We can better think in terms of a kind of "hinge period" in earliest Christianity when the new communities still had very little definition other than the negative identity people gained by being no longer quite what they had been before. The process of conversion produced a sense of being someone new even before there was a concrete, established Christian identity for the newcomer to adopt. The first converts had to begin defining that identity in positive as well as negative terms.

In this way, over a period of centuries, Christianity took shape as a human community with religious institutions—the church. One cannot really say that the church happened first and then created its institutions, for it is impossible to have a community without institutions of some sort—even if they are fairly simple and tentative. Whatever is done once becomes a potential precedent; whatever is done twice is already a tradition of a kind, especially in settings without distinctive traditions already in place. It would be more precise to say that the church is a community whose life came to expression, over a period of time, in a complex of institutions.

The priority of the community over its institutions, however, is a real one, even if it is not precisely temporal—as though the community had existed first, in ideal purity, without any institutions at all.[3] All four of the institutions highlighted by the Chicago-Lambeth Quadrilateral are in some sense creations of the church. Two of them, to be sure, may be thought of as older than the church—the sacraments and some of the scriptures. But even so, the church exercised its freedom in shaping and remodeling them. The gospel accounts say that the two great sacraments were instituted by Jesus himself. Yet the manner of their administration underwent substantial development even within the first century of the church's existence with regard to such matters as who might participate (could Gentiles be baptized?), what name should be invoked in baptism (that of Jesus or that of the Trinity?), whether the rites of bread and wine could be detached from the community meal, and what form the prayer over them should then take.

As for scriptures, the church did inherit some of these from Israel (admittedly, without ever agreeing on a final definition of the canon). Yet the church on its own created an additional canon from its own early writings, to which it soon gave interpretive priority. In one sense, these New Testament writings can be seen as prior to the church that canonized them, since the process of canonization took centuries. Some of them (at least the genuine letters of Paul) derive from the first few decades of the church's existence; others (the gospels) give us some insight into the power of Jesus' life and teaching that gave rise to the church. Even so, the church defined the canonical status of these writings in a long and complex process of building consensus. It might even be said that the consensus is still not complete, since certain "oriental" churches never accepted the New Testament canon exactly as defined by the Mediterranean-derived "mainstream" of Christianity.

Similarly, the doctrines of the creeds have foundations in scripture. They are not *de novo* creations of the church. Yet the selection of doctrines found in the creeds, the precise direction their development took, the exact language chosen for them—all of these represent church responses to theological conflicts of the second and later centuries, and the texts themselves are clearly church products. Their characteristic emphasis on God as creator and on Jesus' incarnation was forged in the Gnostic controversies of the second and third centuries. And the fourth-century Nicene Creed was long controversial for its use of nonbiblical language as well as for other reasons.

In just the same way, the ordained ministry had antecedents in the ministry of Jesus himself, specifically in his reported practice of designating particular groups of disciples (the Twelve and the Seventy) to represent him. Yet the form of ordained ministry that became universal by the end of the second century is clearly a creation of the church, developed over a period of a century and more. It involved the combination of two basic and originally independent elements: one was a threefold order of bishops, presbyters, and deacons, each order with a fairly well-defined identity; the other was an emphasis on legitimate succession, whether conceived in terms of appointment, succession in office, or (in due course) succession through laying on of hands.

There was a time when Anglicans would have denied the element of historical development in the classical model of orders and insisted that this and only this form of ministry was sanctioned by the documents of the New Testament itself. Seventeenth-century Anglican polemicists attacking presbyterian and congregational polities, in a setting where differences about church polity were considered grounds for anathematization, persecution, and civil war, held strongly to this position. Calmer scholarly reflection, made possible by the more irenic conditions of the eighteenth and nineteenth centuries, has found no persuasive evidence of the claim.[4]

Indeed, students of the subject now generally agree that the church had no single institutionalized pattern of ordained ministry in the first century or so of its existence. The first clear evidence for the importance of historic succession is found in the letter called *First Clement,* which probably dates from the last decade of the first century. In it (42:4), Clement of Rome argues that the Corinthian church had acted wrongly in deposing its leaders precisely because they held their positions in due succession to the apostles who founded the church at Corinth.[5] The first unambiguous evidence for a ministry of three orders is found in the genuine letters of Ignatius of Antioch about twenty years later. General acceptance of threefold ministry in historic succession as the standard pattern for churches of the Christian mainstream was probably completed no earlier than A.D. 180.

The early church exercised substantial freedom with respect to all its institutions—at the very least, freedom to remake and regularize them if not to create them from scratch. It is this freedom that I intend when I say that the church has priority over its institutions, including the ordained ministry. Yet the church properly enjoys this priority only insofar as the church itself acknowledges the priority of the gospel over its own existence. A church that proclaims only itself, as opposed to proclaiming the gospel, has no claim on the loyalty of Christians. Nor do its institutions. If the institutions become ends in themselves rather than means of proclaiming the good news, they must either be rescued or, if that is truly impossible, abandoned.

Under normal circumstances, the church and its institutions do manage to convey the good news. They do it imperfectly, as one must expect of human institutions, even those that are divinely aided; yet they do it. The institutions, then, have value as proclaiming the gospel in a variety of forms: sacraments reenact the good news and apply it to us individually, canonical documents reassert it with the constancy of the written word, creeds focus essential implications, the ordained ministry contributes— what? More of that in a moment.

The point I have been making here is that the ordained ministry should be valued as a tertiary rather than the primary element in Christian faith and life. The good news of Jesus is the only primary element. The church emerges from the good news to celebrate and serve it. The institutions of the church are consistent, predictable, repeatable forms in which the church embodies its life in order to remind us of the good news at the heart of it. In this way, the Chicago-Lambeth Quadrilateral was right, I think, to set the classic form of ordained ministry roughly on a level with the two great sacraments, the scriptures, and the creeds. It does not, however, suggest that a church correctly constructed with these four pillars would somehow be self-authenticating—that it could be free of, valid apart from, or superior to the gospel itself. The gospel alone has intrinsic value for Christians.

ORDAINED MINISTRY IS A SACRAMENT OF THE CHURCH'S LIFE

What, then, is the role of ordained ministry? What makes it worth talking about at all in relation to the unity of Christian people? If it is an impediment to that unity (as it has been), might it not be best simply to dispense with it and clear the ground for the gospel to be heard in its pristine purity? If it has only tertiary importance, why hang onto any particular form of it? Why, indeed, trouble ourselves over the precise forms of Christian institutions at all? Why not be content with the gospel alone?

For better or worse, the gospel has never been and will never be heard in a discarnate or nonsocial form. It is always communicated through persons and therefore through language and other human institutions. Why? Because it is directed to human beings, and no human being is discarnate or nonsocial. We cannot dispense with institutions even if we wish. The point, rather, is to have institutions that offer the best possibilities of communicating the good news and the fewest occasions for an idolatrous confusion of the institution with the reality it communicates.

What, then, does the ordained ministry offer in this regard? One can speak of ordained ministry in a variety of ways. One common way is to speak in terms of functions assigned to the ordained. Ordained persons have fulfilled a variety of important functions in the life of the church over almost two millennia. They have been detailed to preserve tradition, to hand it on, to explain it, to govern, to advise, to counsel, to administer the internal life of the community, to pioneer new missions, to assist those in need, to preach, to teach, and so forth. All of these are functions integral to community life, and all have to be performed in order to keep a community healthy.

In the history of the church, it has often been convenient to assign many or most of these functions to the ordained, but there is no intrinsic necessity behind any one way of apportioning them. Indeed, Christian communities have varied enormously in this regard. Within the history of Anglicanism, for example, bishops have had powers of governance ranging from near autocratic to heavily circumscribed. They have had to share their authority variously with monarchs, other bishops (for example, the bishop of Rome before the Reformation or episcopal synods after), councils of various kinds, and diocesan conventions. In some times and places, they have had secular authority as well as religious; in others, even their religious authority is based primarily on personal prestige rather than office.

These functional variations, however, precisely because they are so common, can hardly point us toward the essential issue involved here. The Chicago-Lambeth Quadrilateral, indeed, refers specifically to the "Historic Episcopate, locally adapted in the methods of its administration to the varying needs of the nations and peoples called of God into the unity of His Church." The phrase "locally adapted" suggests an ordained ministry that might vary enormously in function, but is united by its common incorporation of "bishops" ordained in "historic" succession. Whatever is being stressed as essential here, it is not function.

My presupposition is that the essential issue here is not functional, but sacramental. I shall explore in more detail what I understand by that in the following chapter, but a brief explanation of the value I wish to uphold will be appropriate here. If the ordained ministry deserves any kind of place alongside scripture, creeds, and sacraments as a pillar of the future unity of the church, it must have some intrinsic relation to the gospel as integral as that of the other three. I believe that this relation takes on sacramental form.

I do not mean to return here to an older Anglo-Catholic position which suggests that the ordained ministry exists to "confect" the sacraments. (For one thing, one would be very hard put to account for the diaconate on such a basis.) I mean, rather, that the ordained person is himself or herself a kind of sacramental realization of the life of the church as flowing from the gospel. Sacraments are "outward and visible signs of inward and spiritual grace," that is, a kind of realization of the pattern of grace on the visible, tangible plane in a specific object (in this case, a person).

Anglican tradition does not see orders as a sacrament in the same sense as the two great sacraments instituted by Christ.[6] I think it would be difficult to defend any claim that it is, for the great sacraments relate us to the gospel in a way quite different from anything ordination can do. Baptism takes the news of God's grace of forgiveness and applies it specifically to each individual as a physical guarantee that he or she is included within it. The eucharist takes the news of God's near approach to us in the sacrificial life of Jesus and applies it to the gathered community as a guarantee that we are included in that death and resurrection which leads to life. Ordination, on the other hand, can give no additional assurance of good news to the person ordained, for there is no more to give.

The sacramental aspect of ordination does not render the person being ordained more "saved." Rather, it makes of that person a sacramental realization of the gospel life of the church. The church ordains a limited number of persons so that they can mirror the life of the church in such a way as to focus and sharpen the image and then represent it to the church at large in a form that can help all Christians identify its outlines in their own lives. If there is any specific value to any given pattern of ordinations, the classic or any other variant, it must lie in its ability to mirror something of central importance in the gospel life in a way that illumines our everyday living of that life.

Ministerial *function* is thus a matter of almost infinite malleability. From an Anglican perspective, I do not think any one way of deploying the classic three orders can be taken as belonging to their essence. The essential matter in hand here is the *sacramental* aspect of ordination—that is, the way in which ordination makes persons sacraments of gospel life in the church. It is on that basis that I want to argue the value of the historic episcopate.

THE FOUR NOTES OF THE CHURCH
ARE MANIFEST IN ITS MINISTRY

If ordained ministry is indeed a sacrament of the church's life in the gospel, then it ought to correspond in fundamental ways to the church's basic character. From antiquity, this character has traditionally been summed up in the four "notes" of the church: namely, that it is *one, holy, catholic,* and *apostolic.* On the sacramental plane, I believe it is necessary for ordained ministry to relate seriously to each of these elements.

We are already aware of how difficult it is to relate ordination as it now exists to the prospect of *unity.* Both the church and its ministry are fragmented. There are and may always be some people who "resolve" this problem by saying that only their church and their ministry are real; thus, for them, there is no problem about unity. The results of such a claim are more destructive to those who make it than to those against whom it is made. To arrogate to oneself the private possession of the gospel is to show that one has, in fact, no sense at all of what the gospel is about. The claim that any one group is uniquely privileged before God can never find its basis in the gospel of free forgiveness; it can only arise from some claim in law—a claim to superior virtue or correctness as establishing favor with God.

There are few things more fraught with danger to the soul than applying the name of gospel to what is in fact an expression of law. In doing so, we hide from ourselves the very fact that there *is* a gospel, a message about the power of God's forgiveness that could free us from our enslavement to rules, to self-vindication, and

therefore to sin. In the process, the gospel can free us from judg-
mentalism or contempt for our neighbor, including, one hopes,
our sister or brother Christian. There is no place in the gospel for
claiming unique privilege. The simple fact of the matter is that the
church is in fragments, and its ministry is equally in fragments.
No fragment is perfect. Each needs the others in order to become
complete. It will not be possible to reunite the fragments of the
church without reuniting the fragments that make a sacrament of
its life—the ministry.

Any such project of restoring unity must proceed on the basis
of mutual love, that is, a genuine and unforced reverence for one
another. All Christians ought to be glad to find in one another the
evidence of God's grace at work, proclaimed in the word of scripture and preaching, the sacraments of baptism and eucharist, the
daily life of faithful people. And finding these things, we should
have no difficulty in acknowledging each other's communities as
churches. Where there is church, there is also ministry. It is almost
as grave a charge to suggest that a Christian community is without
ministry as to suggest that it is without gospel. Such a judgment
can be leveled at a community only if it is shown to be proclaiming
as its message something other than good news. Even then, it can
only be made reluctantly. In a similar way, Christian ministry
ceases to exist only if it embodies something other than gospel life
in the church.

In the present state of the church, however, ministries are nat-
urally less than fully interchangeable. Recognizing the fact of
ministry in another Christian community does not mean acknowledging it as being exactly identical to ministry in my Christian
community. Whether it is or is not is matter for examination, discussion, and conscientious decision. The ordained ministry is valuable enough in its sacramental role to deserve such careful
consideration—and powerful enough that skating over the difficulties is likely to create further problems down the ecumenical
road.

What is required is a sense of ordained ministry as potentially a
sacrament of the church's unity. To achieve this, we must look
forward to the unity we hope to see renewed among us and not
just backward to the unity we have lost or the historical events by

which we lost it. The classic model of orders was devised in antiquity partly to discourage schism in the church. This was a worthy endeavor, but it has its limits. The ancient rules are incapable by themselves of helping us restore the unity they were designed to protect. It is one thing to say to a person who has fomented division within the congregation and emerged as leader of a breakaway group: "You are committing the sin of schism. You are no true minister of the gospel." It is quite another to say the same to the great-grandchildren of his followers, to people who have never even heard the gospel in any context other than the community the original "schismatic" founded.

Even the most conservative of Anglo-Catholics can afford to recognize that the position of a modern American Methodist is quite different from that of John Wesley. Perhaps one could argue from the perspective of the classical model of orders that Wesley was wrong to ordain irregularly. (On the other hand, one must also acknowledge that he was faced with the inability or unwillingness of the responsible authorities to take appropriate action.) One's judgment of Wesley, however, has little or nothing to do with one's judgment of his twentieth-century successors in another land. Modern American United Methodists are not Anglican schismatics; to describe them as such is meaningless. They are simply another related Christian tradition. An approach to unity, therefore, which only looks backward in an effort to apportion blame or to play out rules that were originally created to prevent schism rather than to restore unity, is bound to fail. Worse than that, it leads to the hypocrisy of suggesting that some streams of Christian tradition are "pure" while others are uniquely tainted with schism.

The unity of the church is a part of its constitution, but has always been problematic in practice. The failure of Christians to maintain a loving unity among themselves is a reproach to the gospel, since it suggests that the gospel has, in fact, little constructive effect on the behavior of those who claim to believe and proclaim it. Yet divisive tendencies have been apparent from the first, as becomes clear from the letters of Paul. Some of these emerged as differences of belief, others as rivalry over leadership. In either case, Paul's letters and those of other early Christian writers are constantly pleading for humility and peaceableness so that each community can maintain internal unity and also remain connected with congregations elsewhere.

The unity of the church does not have to take one particular form. In the twentieth century, schemes of church union have usually stressed the consolidation of overlapping administrative units and the merging of church bureaucracies. This is perhaps not exactly what Jesus had in mind when he prayed that his followers might all be one. At its worst, it feeds the widespread but deeply erroneous notion that "the church" is a certain structure of administrative and theological authorities located in a building somewhere—whether the Vatican in Rome, or the "Blue Vatican" in Springfield, Missouri, or 815 Second Avenue in New York, or wherever.

One might argue that, in the modern world, a monolithic structure for Christianity is neither possible nor desirable. The eras of our greatest unity have not necessarily been the ones of which we should be proudest. Sometimes they have also been times of tyranny and repression. The church has often abused monopoly status. There are excellent grounds for distrusting the church when it becomes too powerful; and a tradition of such distrust, long part of American civic culture, has contributed substantially to human freedom in the twentieth century.

At the same time, the various church traditions, as long as they are divided from one another by suspicion and distrust, are a barrier to the proclamation of the gospel. While the unification of bureaucracies or the remapping and merging of administrative districts may not, in all cases, be desirable, we must seek growth in mutual reverence, love, communication, consultation, and cooperation. Only in this way can Christians begin to treat one another as Christians. An ordained ministry that is a sacrament of gospel life must be able to contribute to this process.

The second note of the church is *holiness*. Probably no aspect of the gospel is so little understood as this. From earliest times, both in Israel and in other cultures, people have tended to equate holiness with purity. One of the distinctive things about the good news of Jesus is that it detaches these two things from one another. In the religion of Israel, to be holy meant to be removed from the ordinary, everyday world and set apart in a special place (a sanctuary) or time (a day of religious obligation). In order to approach the holy with safety, one had to make oneself worthy, putting some separation between one's own daily existence and the sacred sphere one was preparing to enter. One did this by means of avoidance or, where that failed, purification. In Israel, this meant avoidance of such things as menstrual blood (or menstruating women), certain categories of sexual intercourse (in a few cases, all sexual intercourse), various unclean foods, certain unclean fabrics and agricultural practices, nakedness, leprosy, and above all, contact with corpses.

The priests of the Temple had to maintain a high state of purity, and some laypersons, such as the Pharisees, committed themselves to do the same. Ordinary Israelites were usually content with a lesser level of attainment, which made them relatively impure (or "dirty," as we would now say) and excluded them from the holy. Gentiles were dirty by definition since they did not even know the law of purity, much less have any motivation for keeping it.

Jesus, in contrast, brought together the clean and the unclean in his following. He welcomed both those who were worthy to approach the holy, according to the law of Israel, and those who were not; indeed, he sought the latter out. Though Jesus had little occasion for interaction with Gentiles, he seems to have treated them as people of worth. In the decades after Jesus' death and resurrection, his followers, with much pain and hesitation, determined that his gospel was in fact fully available even to unclean Gentiles, and that they did not have to cease being Gentiles in order to receive it.

Thus, whatever the holiness of the church is about, it is clearly not identical with some purity code. There have been repeated efforts over many centuries to redefine the church as a community bounded by purity codes, but all such efforts are radically opposed to the gospel. The church's holiness derives not from its own purity, but from another source altogether—a source to which the physical purity codes are entirely irrelevant.

The church's holiness is a gift given to it directly by God in the good news itself. The church is holy only insofar as it proclaims the good news of open access to God. Otherwise, even if it were composed entirely of vegetarian virgins wearing unmixed natural fibers and miraculously preserved from menstruation, wet dreams, and contact with corpses, it would have no holiness in the specifically Christian sense at all. As Paul puts it, "Christ Jesus . . . has become for us wisdom from God, and also righteousness and holiness and redemption" (1 Cor. 1:30). The church is holy because it embodies Christ and embodies the proclamation of the good news, not because of any purity of its own.

This means that the ordained ministry, if it is to embody the church's holiness in a sacramental way, must reflect not the narrowness, separateness, defensive quality, and aloofness of purity codes, but rather the expansiveness, openness, and accessibility of the good news itself. Our understanding of ordination in the ecumenical context, if it is to be a gospel understanding, must eschew all triumphalism. We must give up trying to prove that one tradition is better or more God-pleasing than another. We cannot claim superiority for one group of Christians over another on the basis of purity of succession, for the holiness of the gospel is not based on purity.

We must also avoid yielding to the great central anxiety of all purity codes, namely, the fear of pollution. The gospel is not afraid of pollution because its good news is more powerful than any danger of contamination. That is why Jesus could eat with publicans and sinners, touch corpses in raising them from the dead or lepers in healing them, permit the woman with the hemorrhage to touch him without reproaching her, and entrust major revelations to a Samaritan woman of ill repute. Christian churches do not have to worry about protecting their ministries from pollution by the ministries of other churches. It is a fear unworthy of people who have heard the gospel.

This does not mean that there are no problems. Ordination and ministerial succession mean something, and we have to choose what we wish to say through them. We have to make sense of them in the ecumenical context. Plunging ahead without trying to understand the language we are using or without deciding what we want to say is no virtue. Fear of contamination, however, of becoming somehow less acceptable to God, ought not to be a concern for us.

The church's holiness is a gift from God. It is, in fact, identical with the gift of Jesus. If it can be lost at all, it will be lost by betrayal of the good news, not by incidental forms of worldly contamination. If it were otherwise, Jesus ought not to have set us the example of associating with the unclean or impure, and the primitive church ought not to have risked admitting those of us who are Gentiles to its membership.

The third note of the church is *catholicity*, by which I understand the church's broad and inclusive extent across time and space. To be catholic means to embrace people of many ages, many places, many tribes, nations, ethnic and linguistic groups, social strata, educational levels, manners of life, pieties, and traditions. It is the obverse of the church's unity, ensuring that that unity does not degenerate into lifeless uniformity; and it is the corollary of the church's holiness, for the variety of life within the church results from God's gracious act of becoming present in holiness to all people without regard to their state of purity.

The present fragmentation of Christian communities is a barrier to realizing the church's full catholicity. Anglicans are accustomed to distinguish certain churches as "catholic," namely, those that have been reluctant to make radical changes and are therefore typically more "traditional" and "liturgical." Yet there is no community in Christianity that is not cut off from some portion of the Christian past and present by the simple fact that it does not share the communion of other Christian communities. No existing community is perfectly catholic.

The restoration of unity, if it proceeds with appropriate respect for the diversity of the Christian faithful, will therefore also be, above all, a restoration of catholicity. This has important consequences for the matter of ordination. An ordained ministry that can sacramentally focus the catholicity of the church will somehow have to reflect the whole history of the divided church. One implication of this is that it must include the classic model: a threefold ministry in historic succession. Since this has been the dominant pattern for most Christians for almost all of Christian history, its absence would be a deep wound to the church's catholicity.

At the same time, a mere substitution of the classic pattern for other types of ordained ministries will not do the job either. In fact, that would result in abandonment of other significant segments of the Christian past and the loss of other aspects of catholicity. It is not only the churches with nonepiscopal ministries or with successions other than the one we call "historic" who ought to resist the loss of their ministries. It would be a diminution of catholicity from which all would suffer. Catholicity not only permits but delights in the diversity of Christians, provided that the diversity coexists with and enriches unity.

The fourth and final note of the church is *apostolicity*. This note derives from an element integral to the good news from the beginning, namely, that it is sent out through *people;* its bearers were not words on a page nor words memorized verbatim, but living, transformed individuals. Jesus could have written books and was undoubtedly aware that some religious leaders of his time did publish their thoughts in such a way—often writing under the names of various ancient worthies. Instead, he chose a particular kind of oral transmission. The oral transmission he chose may have involved some memorizing of his message, but the evidence for memorization is not especially good. The evidence is better for his use of another mode of oral transmission, described by scholars as "composition in performance." In this mode, the bearer of the tradition internalizes the tradition in such a way that he or she can recreate it each time in a form adapted specifically to the audience and the occasion.

Jesus created apostles by confronting people with the good news in the hope that it would transform them. (This was not automatic, as the case of Judas demonstrates.) Then he sent the transformed persons out to do the same with other people. This method combined coherence with tremendous flexibility. A message memorized word for word probably would not have helped Jesus' apostles through the decisive issues they encountered after his death, particularly the question of whether Gentiles could be admitted to baptism as Gentiles. They would have searched the exact words of the tradition in vain for guidance. It was rather their personal experience of the gospel that enabled them to break with convention and make new departures.[7]

What Jesus created, then, was not a set of theological principles or moral rules, but a chain of people transformed by good news and therefore dealing with the world in a new way based on that news. The apostolic element in Christianity is precisely this interpenetration of transformative message and experience in a chain of hearing and proclamation. It implies that Christianity exists basically as a living (not fixed) tradition, forever being passed on from person to person. We meet the gospel in the life and words of others, and others, in turn, meet it in our own.

Luke seems to have limited the term "apostle" mostly to the members of the Twelve. In one sense, this is useful, since it underscores the importance of long experience with the gospel in authenticating apostleship. The apostle is one who has been with Jesus and the gospel long enough to be transformed. On the other hand, Luke's usage may also encourage the confused and mistaken notion that "apostle" was a title of office, bestowed in some regular and official way by Jesus on a limited number of men. Early Christian usage is decisively against any such conclusion. To be an apostle was not a matter of holding a specific, publicly certified office, but a matter of having been confronted and called by Jesus—often the risen Jesus, as was the case with Paul. Apostles were thus more akin to charismatic figures such as prophets than to the orderly, public, office-based ranks of bishops, presbyters, and deacons.[8]

The bishop, therefore, is not a continuation of the apostles any more than any other ordained ministry is. The apostolicity of the church does not depend on any particular way of constituting the ordained ministry, but on a life steeped in the good news and perennially renewed by being passed on from person to person. The church's apostolicity is identical with the degree to which the good news is alive within us and forever reaching out through our lives to the "Gentiles" who have not yet had the chance to hear it.

Even if ordained ministry does not contain or exhaust the church's apostolicity, however, it can still serve as a sacrament of it. It will do so by judicious use of the motif of succession; it will embody a kind of personal chain that mirrors the apostolic connection. In so doing, it will emphasize for the whole church that we receive what we receive from God primarily through other people, and that we are ourselves bearers of the good news for others.[9]

The presuppositions I have set forth in this chapter are personal ones, but also rather traditional Anglican ones.[10] They have points of contact with both Anglo-Catholic and Evangelical Anglican concerns. They have also been affected by experience in ecumenical conversation. To sum up what I have said: I am presupposing, first, that the ordained ministry is not a primary issue for Christian faith, but subordinate to the good news and to the community that arises in response to the good news; second, that the quality that renders the ordained ministry a vital topic for the ecumenical future of the church is its sacramental, not its functional nature; third, that as the ordained ministry is a sacrament of the church's life, any effort to explain its significance must take account of the traditional notes of the church's life—unity, holiness, catholicity, and apostolicity.

My presuppositions will not be agreeable to every reader. I shall not, however, attempt to argue them further, since it would make this book a good deal longer than any sensible person would want it to be. I believe they are defensible and appropriate—even necessary—and I hope to offer the reader an understanding of ordination in the ecumenical context that will accord with them.

Chapter 3

Ordination as Sacramental Action

SACRAMENTALITY

Even though ordination is not a sacrament of the same order as the two great sacraments of baptism and eucharist, it is most readily understood in sacramental terms. By this I mean that it replicates, with physical means, important realities of the life of faith—specifically, in this particular case, realities of life in the *community* of faith. Sacraments are not unlike verbal language. They convey messages; they point to something beyond themselves; they act as signs, interpreting the meaning of the world around them. Christian sacraments, like the word of the gospel, communicate grace—the good news of God's unconditional forgiveness.

Sacraments differ from verbal language, however, in certain important respects. One is that they combine speech with physical acts, including, in most cases, actual physical contact with sacred persons or objects.[1] In a sense, words are addressed to the air, to the generality, to anyone within hearing or reading distance; but touch addresses itself unmistakably to the specific individual. Ear and eye can take in things at a distance from us; touch takes in only what is in immediate proximity. Sacraments, therefore, make specific applications of universal truths and realize them, in specific rites, in the lives of individuals and of face-to-face communities. One might even say that they transform such persons and bring them into a new status: that of the baptized, that of communicants, and so forth.

A sacrament not only touches persons and transforms their status, it also transforms our perception of the material element or elements that the sacrament uses. Baptism not only changes the baptized; it also changes water, so that henceforth all water has

43

new meaning for the baptized. The eucharist, in the same way, gives new significance to all food. This is already visible in early Christian documents. 1 Pet. 3:20, for instance, can interpret Noah's Flood as a kind of baptism because the experience of baptism transformed the meaning of water for Christians; even at its most destructive, it can still carry a quality of hope. Again, Christians fed by the eucharist could look back at the story of Jesus' feeding of the multitude—or, beyond it, at the manna in the wilderness—and see in it a kind of eucharist before the eucharist (e.g., John 6).

Sacraments are thus dependent on a certain sense of the holiness of the creation itself, a point deeply concordant with what was said about the nature of holiness in the preceding chapter. For Christians, the holy is no longer characterized by its remoteness, separateness, or circumscribed character, but by its graciousness, its openness and availability, indeed by its very ordinariness. Thus all water is potentially water of baptism; all bread and wine is potentially eucharistic bread and wine. The sacredness of the sacramental moment not only chooses out and transforms the person receiving the sacrament, it also reconfirms the grace of creation, saying an "Amen" to God's judgment that the creation is indeed "very good" and reviving in us an appropriate veneration of its goodness in water, in food and drink, and in the whole range of reality implied by them.

The sacraments are like verbal language in that they convey meaning; but they go beyond most uses of verbal language in that they actualize the meaning they convey.[2] Thus the eucharist does not merely talk about the death and resurrection of Jesus, but, in a sacramental fashion, actually makes them present and applies them directly to the assembled faithful, individually and collectively. Hence the belief of most Christians that Jesus is "really present" in the bread and wine of the eucharist. The sacrament offers not only a statement about Jesus, but an encounter with him.

This is not to identify sacramental reality absolutely or unequivocally with the reality it communicates. When sixteenth-century Anglican reformers complained that the doctrine of transubstantiation "overthroweth the nature of a Sacrament," they were objecting to a kind of collapsing of "levels" whereby sacraments ceased to be language at all. They no longer referred beyond themselves and became, instead, privileged moments of direct access to the uncreated or transcendent order—anomalies, as it were, in the boundaries of the space-time continuum.[3] Sacraments, like every aspect of the Christian religion, are truly of this world, however much they also bring us into relationship with God. They ought, therefore, to be intelligible in human terms without any loss of their power to touch us. Sacraments belong, after all, to this age of faith and hope, not to the future age of fulfillment; they must therefore still point to something beyond themselves. They are a language that conveys what it speaks of, and yet remains a language.

This is why sacraments cannot be said to exhaust the reality that they make present on the tangible plane. The real presence of Jesus in the bread and wine of the holy table implies no corresponding "real absence" elsewhere. The assurance of salvation conveyed in baptism implies no corresponding assurance of damnation for the unbaptized. Rather, each sacrament focuses a reality that continues to transcend the sacrament—focuses it in order to apply it specifically to this person or that person, this group or that group. To suppose that the transcendent reality is somehow confined to the sacrament or to those who receive it is to reintroduce a kind of purity code which says that only the baptized or only communicants are pleasing to God, and that no one else has access to God's grace. In that case, there is no more gospel, but only a new set of legally prescribed works by which we ensure our standing before God.

ORDINATION AS SACRAMENT

If we apply these general observations about sacramentality to ordination in particular, what shall we expect to find? As I have already suggested, orders are a sacrament of the church's life in the gospel rather than a sacrament directly of the good news itself. We should expect to find ordained ministry pointing to the reality of the church's ministry—not offering a full and exhaustive embodiment of it, but focusing it in such a way as to draw attention to the holiness and divine power of all gospel ministry and to assure the

local Christian community that it is a community of ministers.
Any limiting of ministry to the ordained, even the assumption
that their ministry is preeminent over or the fountainhead of other
ministries, will be misleading and will "overthrow the nature of a
sacrament."

We shall also expect that the sacramental rites by which ordained ministry is constituted will involve some element of physical contact as well as verbal proclamation. Sacraments speak
through concrete specifics, not generalities. Ordination, therefore, will not be merely a generalized declaration that all Christian
people are ministers of the gospel (though that is in fact true), but
will physically constitute certain persons as sacraments of that
ministry in order to focus the diffuse reality of ministry for the
benefit more of the people of God than of the ordained themselves. Hence the importance of particular persons and of the
physical contact by which they are designated. Only through the
use of particularities can we have sacraments.

At the same time, if sacraments are a kind of language, then the
physical actions of ordination must take place in a context that
enables them to speak clearly. The rite must be purposeful if it is
to allow the ordained to become interpretive images of the ministry of the whole people of God. With other sacraments, modern
study has shown that close attention to the classical rites can repay
us with insight into their meaning. The major elements of the
classical ordination rites can help us understand what all ordination rites signify.

THE CLASSICAL PATTERN OF ORDERS

In defining and studying the significant elements of ordination,
we must avoid falling in with the long-standing tendency among
Christians to try to reduce sacramental rites to an "essence." In
some cases, this has a practical purpose. In cases of emergency, for
example, one wants to know what is the bare minimum that will
constitute the rite of baptism. This information is useful not because God's goodwill toward any person is dependent on the rite
of baptism, but just the reverse: the rite of baptism is dependent
on God's goodwill toward every person. It is important, rather,

because baptism offers a kind of individual actualization of God's goodwill, and one wishes therefore to know when it has in fact happened. It is a concrete personal pronouncement to which I can subsequently return when generalized assurances of God's love for every individual are, as must sometimes be the case, unpersuasive to *me,* here and now.

At other times, the desire to reduce a rite to its minimal ritual essence may arise from questions of piety (e.g., at what point one ought to strive for the most attentive devotion during the eucharist) or of ecclesiastical polemics (e.g., whether one can dismiss the eucharist of another Christian group as inauthentic because it lacks some key ingredient). Such issues as these seem to have been the motive force behind the Western catholic tendency to reduce the "essence" of the eucharist to the words of institution spoken by a properly authorized person over the bread and wine.

Perhaps the single most illuminating development in modern liturgical study has been to scrap this reductionist paradigm of sacramental rites and to replace it with another that stresses a more global, dynamic, and comprehensive approach. This approach does not deny the legitimacy of the simplest form of baptism administered in an emergency situation, but it suggests that the church had reasons for setting baptism, under more usual circumstances, in a larger, richer, and more informative context. Similarly, in the case of the eucharist, it is now usual to understand it not in terms of a minimum that might constitute a "valid" rite, but as a complex action beginning with reading of scripture and proclamation of the gospel and progressing through the fourfold sacramental action of offertory, thanksgiving, fraction, and communion. In both cases, the full-fledged "normal" rite, not its reduced "essence," is the key to understanding.

If we apply a similar paradigm to ordination, we find that, beginning with the *Apostolic Tradition* of Hippolytus (the earliest record we have of actual ordination rites), there is a consistent pattern consisting of four elements:

1. Ordinations take place in the context of the eucharistic assembly, complete with proclamation and sacramental celebration of the gospel.

2. There is an element of choice by the local church or, at the very least, the rite is conducted in the presence of the whole congregation, thus implying popular consent.
3. In the case of bishops, there is ratification of the election by the larger church in that neighboring bishops ordain the new bishop.
4. There is laying on of hands by persons who stand in specified sacramental relationships to the local congregation and/or the larger church, accompanied by prayer.

All elements of this pattern are significant to understanding ordination as a sacramental rite.[4]

What is vital here is not so much the exact details as the general drift. Just as with the eucharist one finds the occasional anomalous prayer of thanksgiving—ancient ones, for example, without the words of institution, or more modern ones without an epiklesis—so with ordination one might find now one, now another element missing without presuming that the whole pattern has been irretrievably lost. The significant thing is that:

1. the gospel is emphasized as the source of ministry;
2. the consent of the people of God is manifest;
3. the local church acts in communion with other Christians, not in a way that would tend to cut them off; and
4. there is an *act,* almost inevitably a tactile act, designating the person who is being ordained.

The tendency to reductionism has often focused on the tactile element in this pattern as if it were the only thing of real significance. If that were accepted, one would need know only a very few things in order to judge the nature of the action. Who touched whom? For what express purpose? For example, some Anglicans might argue that it was enough to know that the first Methodist bishops in the United States were not touched by other bishops in historic succession in order to reach the conclusion that they were not correctly ordained. Or other Anglicans might judge that the Church of Sweden's having preserved an ongoing tactile succession from before the Reformation is enough to make its ordinations "valid." Or Roman Catholics might say that lack of appropriately expressed purpose in the process of laying on hands is sufficient to warrant a negative judgment on Anglican orders.

On the other hand, the more comprehensive view—which, as I have said, is more in accord with current modes of understanding the two great sacraments—would be inclined to look at broader patterns. In particular, one must stress the importance of the eucharist as a setting for ordinations. The case of Rome's negative judgment on Anglican orders in the nineteenth century is a useful example. In it, Anglicans were faulted for wrong "intention." If we look at "intention" in too narrow a sense, however, we have to try to read minds in a rather precise way. How exact and perfect does the implied intention have to be in order to make ordination possible? Can any theological inadequacy whatever, perceived or real, invalidate the act? Or is it enough that a church intends to do what the whole church has always intended to do in this matter?

Surely the intention to do what the church has always done is intention enough. Otherwise almost any theological disagreement would have the power to invalidate ordinations. Evangelicals would have to regard medieval ordinations as invalid because of a faulty theology of eucharistic sacrifice—thus implying that, in fact, no valid succession of ministry had survived in the West to the Reformation. Anglo-Catholics would have to object to all Roman Catholic ordinations because of a faulty and uncatholic understanding of episcopal ministry as flowing from the papacy. And so on. The sacrament of orders would thus become entirely the prisoner of theological interpretation, when the flow ought to be the reverse of that. The sacraments are prior to and persist in the face of all kinds of mistakes and disputes about their meaning. Theology is derivative, representing an effort, always tentative and insufficient, to interpret their significance for a particular community in a particular historical setting.

THE CONTEXT OF WORD AND SACRAMENT

The traditional pattern for ordinations affirms and protects their sacramental character by placing them in a context in which the gospel is proclaimed in word and sacrament, thereby affirming that the local church means to do what the church catholic means to do: effect a sacrament of the gospel at work in the life of the Christian community. This does not mean that variations of detail—for example, with regard to who touches whom in the laying on of hands—are meaningless. But it does put such matters in the larger context of the gospel, thereby potentially saving us from resorting to a rule-bound scrupulosity that ill becomes people who have heard the good news of grace.

It should be possible, instead, to affirm that all ordained ministries carried out with the intent to do what the church catholic does in ordaining are real sacramental ministries. The proof that an ordained ministry conforms to these specifications is the way in which it is associated with the gospel in word and sacrament. Ideally, the ordination itself should take place in the eucharistic context. If, for some reason, local tradition has separated ordinations from their normal setting of word and sacrament, then the local church's employment of the ordained in ministering word and sacrament would still indicate that its intention was to do what the church catholic has so long intended to do. Given this principal, virtually all Christian ordinations must be presumed to be "valid" and authentic. It would be difficult, in fact, to produce an "invalid" ordination.

This acknowledgment does not, of course, resolve all ecumenical difficulties. For Methodists and Anglicans to acknowledge that the ordained ministry of each is indeed a valid sacramental ministry in its own context does not tell us how to bring the two ministries together in the process of bringing the two churches into communion with one another. Even though they are both within the orbit of the church catholic and its intention to ordain persons as sacraments of the ministry of the whole church, they are still different in other significant respects, and therefore they probably "say" something a little different about the self-understanding of the communities that employ them.

Despite the remaining difficulties, however, recognition that ordination is and must always be in the context of the proclamation and celebration of the gospel helps clarify an important issue. It is both unnecessary and inappropriate for Anglicans to suggest, as some of us have at times, that only ministries that match our own rather closely are real sacramental ministries. The validity of orders does not depend on the precise tactile formula in isolation from other elements. The validity of one tradition of orders does not depend on the invalidity of others. For the good order of any Christian community in its communion with its Creator and Redeemer, it is enough that the local church intends to do what the church catholic has intended to do from the start, namely, to create ordained persons as sacraments of the church's shared ministry. No criticism of other churches' ministries is required. What all share is a common and catholic purpose, identified by the shared practice of ordaining in the context of the good news.

THE CONTEXT OF COMMUNITY CHOICE

Implicit in my argument to this point is that a *community* ordains, not just the designated individuals (normally themselves ordained persons) who lay hands on the ordinand. This point is implicit in the ordination rites themselves, though in a way that is sometimes barely noticed. The choice of ordinand, after all, is normally made before the ordination itself through the machinery normal to the given community. The ordinand was seldom, if ever, someone chosen by divine sign, as one might expect in an institution as charismatically inclined as earliest Christianity. The occasional exception, such as Fabian of Rome, tests the rule without damaging it. The Roman Church appears to have been deeply divided and unable to make a normal decision in the episcopal election; and the sign of a dove descending on Fabian was taken as sign of divine election, which in turn led to acclamation by the church.[5] The norm was that the congregation decided, and it did so by the methods normal to the place and time.

In *Apostolic Tradition* 15, Hippolytus even tells us that, in a certain sense, charismatics cannot be ordained. What can the church's rites add to the person chosen by the Spirit? Hippolytus therefore forbids the ordaining of healers as such, since ordination would add nothing to their miraculous charisma. One might also note the case of confessors (those who had suffered for their faith under persecution without actually being killed). In the third century, they could apparently be enrolled among the deacons or presbyters without ordination. They enjoyed a kind of divine election, which rendered ordination superfluous.[6]

Normally speaking, the only persons to be ordained in the early church were those presented by the congregation or, in large churches, presented *to* the congregation for its approval. This did not necessarily mean that all ordinands were chosen by popular vote, which would probably have struck the people of the Roman Empire as an odd way to do things. Only the bishop need normally be chosen (or confirmed) in this way. And the bishop, as corporate head of the body politic, would presumably choose others in consultation with his advisors, the presbyteral college.[7]

In subsequent eras, the mode of indicating the congregation's choice was adapted to the political presuppositions and realities of changing culture. The riots that accompanied the election of Damasus as bishop of Rome were still part of a popular electoral procedure. One can scarcely excuse them, but they are good evidence of the survival of Christian popularism into an era of increasing imperial involvement in the church. On the other hand, the waning of popular institutions after the fall of Rome tended to leave responsibility for election to a local patron (typically a noble), a "chapter" of ecclesiastical officials, or the sometimes tense interplay between the two.

Since such elections were fully in accord with the political presuppositions of the Middle Ages (the ordinary commoner would perhaps have been very surprised to be dragged into the process), they were legitimate ways of selecting those to be ordained. If they gave a certain preference, illegitimate by the standards of the gospel, to the powerful and well connected, that is not fundamentally different in kind from giving the same preference to a popular majority, which may at times prove equally self-interested, narrow, and inadequate to the occasion.

The point, in any case, is that *churches* choose ordinands. In principle, *local* churches choose ordinands, though they may resign that privilege to some degree if they see good reason to do so. Even if all practical control over the process of choosing ordinands has been removed from the local church, the people of God still have left to them the final "vote" of appearing or not appearing at the ordination itself. Though there may be individual exceptions, the norm established for ordinations from the second century onward is that they are acts of the whole Christian community, taking place in the presence of that community. They are not equivalent to the awarding of degrees or the licensing of professionals or any other essentially individual kind of authorization. They are more nearly equivalent to the inauguration of an elected official, which can be private only under most exceptional circumstances.

This essentially communal element in ordination has important consequences for an old quandary that has deviled some forms of Anglican thinking about ordained ministry—the business of *episcopi vagantes,* bishops without authentic Christian communities to which they are related. It is an embarrassment in certain Anglican theories of orders that they require us to take the ordinations of such bishops more seriously than those of settled Christian communities which do not perpetuate the historic episcopate—an extreme case of separating the power of ordination from the life of the gospel. Given the communal nature of ordination, however, it is unthinkable for a bishop to ordain as an independent agent. Missionary bishops may be allowed to do something that looks rather like this, but they are "middle terms," authorized by the community that sent them out and by the fact that they are bringing a new Christian community into being where they labor. The *episcopus vagans,* on the other hand, is a bishop without church and therefore, if the theory I am proposing be accepted, without power to ordain. Ordinations by such bishops should normally be regarded as frivolous imitations of sacraments and not as creating real sacramental ministries.

The act of laying on hands, then, is not the sum total of the process of creating sacramental ministers. At least two circumstantial elements are vital in giving sacramental significance to the act: the proclaiming of the gospel, which indicates that the local church intends to do what the church catholic does in ordaining; and the presence and consent of the local congregation, showing that it is the church that ordains through its ministers, and not the ministers alone, with or without the consent of the church.

THE CONTEXT OF THE LARGER CHURCH

The church which ordains, however, is not simply the local church, however that may be defined. For Anglicans, the local church is probably best understood as the diocese. This is not altogether satisfactory, since our dioceses are not face-to-face communities. By the late second century many metropolitan dioceses were already far too large to function in that way; and later missionary movement into northern and western Europe made for larger and larger dioceses and bishops who were more and more remote from their people. Consequently, the parish came to be the true local church in some sense. Still, for purposes of ordination, the diocese carries on the functions that belonged to it as a manifestation of the local church in, for example, Hippolytus's *Apostolic Tradition.*

At one crucial juncture, however, according to the classic pattern of ordinations, the local church, however defined, had to secure the cooperation of the larger church. For the ordination of a bishop, three bishops were required, meaning that the local church must call on its neighbors to confirm its choice. Failure to confirm (i.e., refusal to ordain) would represent a judgment that the local church had chosen a candidate who threatened the unity of the larger church. The autonomy of the local church was thus always relative, for it could not flout the united judgment of neighboring Christians and still claim to be part of the church catholic.

The requirement that three bishops ordain each new bishop constituted the new bishop as part of a wider network. This arrangement implied a necessary connection between the local church and the church catholic, confirming what was said earlier about ordinations as set in the context of word and sacrament. As there is only one gospel, it was essential that Christians seek to preserve the unity of the gospel community in order to avoid defaming the gospel by unloving behavior. The classical model of orders, by requiring three bishops to ordain a new one, focused this need for unity in a sacramental way in the person of the bishop.

TACTILE SUCCESSION

Finally, the classical model of orders—having stressed the centrality of the gospel, the reality of the local church, and the connection with the church catholic—focused on the ordinand in the act of laying on hands with prayer. The laying on of hands seems to lend itself, if detached from its context, to magical interpretations. Many Christians have thought of the authority of the ordained as a kind of *mana,* a powerful fluid or current that can effect certain miraculous things such as consecrating the elements of the eucharist and dispensing blessings. This power can also be communicated to other persons through the laying on of hands, but only those magically endowed can pass it on through the magic of ordination.

Such an understanding of ordination has the effect of detaching it both from the gospel and from the church. It is thinking of this kind that justifies the ordinations of *episcopi vagantes* as "valid" because they connect a person possessing such power with a person who "correctly" receives it. Such thinking does not respect the importance of gospel faith nor that of authentic Christian community, with the result that orders become a kind of self-perpetuating machine for ordinations with no intrinsic relationship to gospel or church. Conversely, a gathering of Christians who proclaim and live by the gospel in its utmost purity, if they had not inherited the right "touch" would, by this magical thinking, have no real ministry at all. If this thinking were correct, then the whole system of ordained ministry would be essentially non-Christian and could have no serious claim on the attention of believers. Such a ministry would rest on an authority independent of or merely parallel to that of the good news.

This is an extreme misinterpretation, however, of the meaning of the laying on of hands, produced by isolating it from the other elements normal to the sacrament of orders. When we understand that the laying on of hands can itself only proceed rightly in the context of word and sacrament, with the consent of the local church and in communion with the larger church, we shall also understand that the laying on of hands is not an isolated, amoral, detached, magical work performed by the ordaining clergy, but rather an act of the whole church, under the gospel, through its sacramental ministers. It is not a magical but a designating act, giving to the ordained a certain sacramental ministry, that is, a ministry that is sacramental of the ongoing ministry of the whole church.

In the following chapter, I shall look more closely at the act of laying on hands in order to establish more clearly why it is an act full of sacramental rather than magical power. I shall also examine the particulars of how the laying on of hands is conducted, according to the classic model of Christian ordinations, in order to discern what messages about the church and its ordained ministry are incorporated in it.

As a sacramental act, ordination is a kind of language. In it, churches speak about their own life under the gospel. But sacraments are also more than language, and ordination not only tells about the church but constitutes certain persons as sacraments of the life of the church. These sacramental persons are defined by the context of the gospel, by the choice of the local church, and by the consent of the larger church. The laying on of hands embodies all this in a sacramental act of touching.

Chapter 4

Laying on of Hands

ON THE ONE HAND, IT IS EASY TO MISUNDERSTAND THE LAYING ON of hands as a magical act. On the other, it is equally tempting to dismiss the laying on of hands as mere formalism. As long as a person has been clearly and publicly designated as an official minister of the gospel in the church, can it really make any difference who has laid hands on the person, or even whether hands have been laid on at all? In one sense, I have been arguing that it makes no difference. As long as the people of a particular Christian community are agreed that they designate their official ministry in a certain way—say, by formal proclamation, by licensing, or by some other symbolic gesture, such as the handing over of a Bible or another sacred object—then the minister so designated has full authority in and for that group of Christians.

This does not, however, mean that laying on of hands is unimportant or unworthy of careful reflection. Like every ritual gesture, it is rich in meaning. Whether we wish to or not, we must make choices among the possible meanings. For one thing, no single Christian community really exists in isolation. Insofar as we are attentive to Jesus' prayer for unity among his followers, we must at least begin to reflect on what our ministries say about our future communion with one another. For another, the act of touching, of which the laying on of hands is a kind of subcategory, is by no means trivial in itself. To the contrary, it has a rich and wide range of meanings in human experience, specifically in Israelite and Christian tradition. Many of these meanings come into play when it is used in rites of ordination.

Like the water used in baptism and the food and drink used in the eucharist, touching evokes a range of associations and meanings and thereby gives a certain power to the sacrament with

57

which it is associated. Touch may be loving, supportive, hostile, sympathetic, contaminating, inquiring, pleading, threatening, and so forth. In any given instance, the context and the manner of touching serve to convey its particular significance in that moment. And yet the power of touch to communicate any one of these things intensely and personally must surely lie partly in the fact that it can communicate them all. In other words, touch is a rich language capable of conveying many different things. We ought, therefore, to take it as seriously as other forms of human communication.

SCRIPTURAL MEANINGS

In the scriptures of Israel and the church, we find a complex and varied sense of the power of hands and of touching. Even the subcategory "laying on of hands" has a surprisingly broad range of meanings.

The term *yad* ("hand"), in Hebrew, designates a person's exercise of active power. This was a normal idiom in biblical Hebrew. A relatively literal English translation of the scriptures of Israel is full of references to the hand. These sound poetic and metaphorical to the English-speaking person but were normal idiom in the original tongue. People "put forth their hand" to do things, their affairs "prosper in their hands," they are "delivered out of the hand of their enemies," their "hand is triumphant," and so forth. In a similarly personal fashion, God saves the people "with a mighty hand and outstretched arm"; and the creation is "the work of God's hands."

It would overload this study if we attempted a detailed or comprehensive discussion of the scriptural associations of hands and touch; but it should be worthwhile to explore briefly some aspects clearly relevant to the rites of ordination. The touch of hands can convey blessing, as in the blessing Jacob gave to the sons of Joseph (Gen. 48:8–22); even the lifting up of the hands can do so, as in the case of Aaron's high-priestly blessing (Lev. 9:22). In their consecration, priests of Israel were touched with blood and had the offerings placed in their hands (Lev. 8:22–29). One Hebrew idiom for "consecrate" translates literally as "fill the hands."[1]

Laying on of hands had a particular role to play in the offering of certain sacrifices. The Israelite who brought a burnt offering was to lay his hand on it before slaughtering it in the presence of the priest so that it would be accepted as atonement (Lev. 1:1–5). The same act was required in making a peace offering (3:1–2) or a sin offering (4:4, 15, 24, 29, 33), though no explicit link to atonement is made in these cases. In the case of the scapegoat, which was taken into the wilderness rather than sacrificed at the altar, the high priest was to lay both hands on the animal and confess the sins of the people, thus "putting them on the head of the goat" and sending them away (16:20–22).

In these sacrificial examples, the laying on of one or both hands seemed to achieve several things: it identified the animal as belonging to the person who sacrificed it; it established a direct ceremonial connection between the two beings; it even transferred to the animal some aspect of the owner's identity so that the animal's death could reestablish concord between the sacrificer and God, or so that the animal could embody and carry away the sins confessed over it. Various theories or theologies of sacrifice could be spun out to account for these things, but perhaps (as is often said to be the rule in matters ritual) the acts are older than the explanations. In making sacrifice, the worshiper meant to be offering to the deity something of himself or herself. The ceremony of touching the animal on the head served to indicate this concretely and powerfully without an excess of explanatory detail.

Thus far we have been looking at positive meanings of touch, but it would be misleading if we did not observe that, in the religion of ancient Israel, touch was at least equally capable of communicating negative qualities. Since impurity was seen as a kind of physical reality, highly contagious and easily communicable, touching was a risky business. Touching something unclean could render one unclean. Whether one intended to "commit" uncleanness, or even knew that one had done so, was irrelevant (Lev. 5:2–3). Impurity had an intrinsic power to soil whatever came into contact with it.

It may be difficult for modern Gentile Christians to understand the far-reaching importance of the purity code in the time of Jesus. In origin, the purity code probably aimed at making people aware of God's holiness and giving them ways to approach the holy. In due course, however, it got turned on its head and, from being a means of access to the holy, it became a means of excluding the unclean. To be impure or unclean meant that one was alienated from God, barred from the sanctuary, and socially inferior. This is why Jesus attacked the purity code and bracketed it as irrelevant. He did not forbid its observance, but he did forbid us to judge others because they were unclean, impure, dirty.[2]

Indeed, Jesus effectively reversed the "flow" that purity law assumed in the case of touch. Where purity law assumed that the unclean always overpowers the clean and contaminates it, Jesus behaved as if the opposite were true—at least in his own case. Lepers were contagious of uncleanness; hence the law that required them to dress distinctively and warn people off (Lev. 13:45–46). Jesus, however, touched a leper, with the consequence that the leper was rendered clean instead of Jesus' being rendered unclean (Mark 1:40–45). Again, menstruating women were unclean. Yet when a woman who had been hemorrhaging (and therefore was legally menstrual) touched Jesus, she was healed; and he himself praised rather than rebuked her (Mark 5:25–34). Again, corpses were unclean; indeed, they presented the single most virulent threat of contagion (Num. 19:11–19). Yet Jesus apparently touched a corpse in the act of raising the daughter of Jairus from the dead (Mark 5:41).[3]

This dialectic of purity and impurity in the act of touching is not merely an interesting bit of antiquarian information; it is directly relevant to the modern ecumenical discussion of ordination. Often, anxieties about preserving the purity of existing ministries impede discussions of how we might move toward future unity. Yet the witness of Jesus' own life and work is that the gospel is more powerful than impurity and that Christians need no longer fear the contagious virulence of dirt. While Jesus did not forbid private practice of existing purity codes, he did forbid any sort of commitment to them or understanding of them that could foster a contemptuous, judgmental, or exclusive attitude toward others.

It is important, then, in the modern situation, to recognize the ongoing power of purity codes, written or unwritten, conscious or not, because they will inevitably have an effect on the ways in which we respond to or evaluate a ceremony that involves certain persons touching certain others in a significant way. The "natural" human attitude will detect in such events a grave danger of contamination, against which piety must mount vigilant guard in order to keep alien filth at bay. Only minds and hearts transformed by the news of God's power and goodness can see in the mingling of diverse Christian successions a triumph of the gospel rather than the loss of purity.

Finally, we might note the role of touch in making people sick (e.g., the lameness of Jacob, Gen. 32:25) or well (e.g., the blind man of Bethsaida, Mark 8:22–26). We might also speak of the hand of God as a source either of protection or disaster (e.g., Isa. 25:10–12, where it brings protection to Jerusalem and disaster to Moab). Here, too, as in the case of purity, the significant thing for our purpose is that Jesus defined the predominant "current" of touch as positive rather than negative. God touches us for healing and protection, even if it does not always seem so in our eyes.

THE BEGINNINGS OF ORDINATION

The whole range of meanings ascribed to touch in scripture is potentially relevant to the question of ordination. Of particular importance, however, is language in the New Testament that may shed light on the beginnings of the actual Christian practice of ordination. Early Christians practiced laying on of hands for a variety of purposes: for healing, as when Ananias laid hands on Saul and cured the blindness that had struck him on the road to Damascus (Acts 9:10–19); or as an aspect of Christian initiation, as when Paul laid his hands on some disciples of John the Baptist and they received the Spirit (Acts 19:1–7);[4] or to impart blessing to a particular project, as when the prophets and teachers of Antioch, in obedience to a command of the Spirit, set Barnabas and Saul apart for a particular mission with fasting, prayer, and laying on of hands (Acts 13:1–3).

Despite superficial similarities, this last example should not really be thought of as an "ordination." In his letters, Paul never refers to the Antiochian experience but regards his own authority as an immediate, charismatic fact founded on his having been called to his particular mission by the risen Lord. Moreover, Luke's specific language in Acts 13 suggests that he saw Barnabas and Saul as being set apart for a particular task (*ergon*) rather than instituted in an office.[5]

Something similar may well be going on in the case of the Board of Seven in Acts 6:1–7. Luke presents them as people charged with a certain task connected with the church's welfare program. Reading between the lines, one can see that the members of this board must have exercised other kinds of leadership in the community as well; and membership on a board is a kind of official status. (In the Latin-speaking world, they would no doubt have held the title *septemviri*.) Still, the laying on of hands in this case is analogous to what Luke relates in Acts 13—and probably not different in any fundamental way from Jesus' blessing of the children (Matt. 19:13) or from the use of the same gesture in connection with baptism. Among the earliest Christians, laying on of hands had not yet been differentiated, as it would later be, into distinct rites of confirmation, ordination, and lesser blessings.

Only in some very late New Testament documents do we have reference to laying on of hands in a way that sounds unambiguously like ordination. In the early second century, the author of the Pastoral Epistles (1 and 2 Timothy, Titus), writing under the name of Paul, was seeking to regularize the community life of Christian congregations. One way of doing this was to make the leadership of the congregations more regular and predictable. The author wanted local leaders to be selected with care and designated clearly. Only responsible people were to be chosen, and they were then to be given clear authority and responsibility in the church. In this context, the older practice of laying on hands for all kinds of new undertakings took on a new, more deliberately institutional significance.[6]

In addressing "Timothy," the author emphasizes that the younger man's role, as a kind of apostolic delegate in Ephesus, is to appoint reliable people to positions of responsibility. In doing so, Timothy must exercise caution, carefully evaluating the respectability of candidates. He must not rush matters; if he makes a mistake through lack of consideration, he will be responsible for it. "Lay hands[7] quickly on no one, and don't share in other people's sins. Keep yourself dedicated" (1 Tim. 5:22).

The authority that "Timothy" was to convey to the persons he appointed was the same authority that had been given to him in a similar fashion. While waiting for Paul to return to Ephesus, he is to keep busy with reading, preaching, and teaching. Moreover, writes the author, "Do not neglect the gift that is in you, which was given you through prophecy with laying on of the hands of the college of elders (or presbyters)" (1 Tim. 4:14). Here the gift (*charisma*) comes directly from the Spirit through prophecy. At the same time, it is accompanied by or occurs in the context of the laying on of hands by an authoritative body.

In another passage, the author writes a little differently about this event (if, indeed, he conceived it as the same event in Timothy's "biography"): "I am reminding you to rekindle the gift (*charisma*) of God, which is in you through the laying on of my hands" (2 Tim. 1:6). Here the *charisma* is no longer something given directly by the Spirit, but something transferred through a sacramental gesture. And unless the author is merely speaking in a kind of shorthand, he regarded the gesture in itself as sufficient to ensure its transmission. This language suggests the transmission of some kind of public authority or status—something that "Paul" had and had the power to transmit to "Timothy."

Thus only in late New Testament writings do we find possible reference to rites of ordination as distinct from the earlier and more general use of laying on of hands. No doubt some earlier layings on of hands were subsequently reinterpreted as ordinations, and we may even see this process at work in the Pastoral Epistles. Whereas the statement about Timothy's experience in 1 Timothy is consistent with the earlier, more general usage, the one in 2 Timothy would find a more comfortable home in the context of an actual ordination rite. If the author really conceived these experiences as referring to the same event, a process of reinterpretation has taken place between the writing of the first and second letter.[8]

In any case, the evidence shows us a process by which the generalized practice of the laying on of hands was becoming focused, in part, into a rite of ordination. This was linked to (but not identical with) an ongoing search on the part of early Christians for stable models of community life. As laying on of hands came to be the broadly accepted means by which the church designated authoritative officeholders, it brought with it the power of its own broad and varied communicative potential—the whole range of meanings and associations inherited from the long tradition of Israel and modified by the witness of Jesus' life and teaching. The church took all of these opportunities and challenges and fashioned from them a coherent system of touching persons in order to commission them to sacramental office.

THE THREE ORDERS

Early in the second century, the classic model of ordained ministry, consisting of three orders, began to take shape; by the end of that century, it was essentially universal among Christians. Ordination to each of the three orders was governed by a slightly but significantly different formula. A comparison of the three formulae reveals much about the meaning of each of the three orders and of ordination in general.

The pattern, first recorded in Hippolytus's *Apostolic Tradition*, is this: a bishop is ordained by three other bishops; a presbyter is ordained by the local bishop, with the local presbytery also laying on hands; a deacon is ordained by the local bishop alone. By altering the prescription for who laid hands on whom, the early churches were able to say a great deal not only about the orders of ordained ministry and how they related to one another, but also about the nature of the church that these orders expressed sacramentally.

Clearly, the figure of the bishop was central to the system since at least one bishop was required for every kind of ordination. If we look for the reason behind this, we shall find it in the fact that the bishop was the center of unity in the local church. The argument Ignatius of Antioch made for the importance and value of bishops was that only a single leader could function to hold a divisive congregation together. "Do nothing without the bishop!"—his repeated cry[9]—was less a claim to power than an effort to hold together communities that seemed bent on endless fragmentation.

The fact that the ancient bishop was elected by the local congregation and ordained in its presence was sufficient guarantee that he at least began his work with the cooperation and consent of the community itself. The presence of three neighboring bishops to ordain him was a sign of his being accepted by a larger network of Christian communities so that he could be a bond and sign of unity between his own local church and the church catholic. The bishop was thus the sacramental focus for the church's unity both locally and ecumenically; and the provisions for his ordination were designed to embody precisely this reality.[10]

The local bishop, in ordaining a deacon, was the only person to lay hands on the ordinand. Since the ordinations of deacons were as public as those of bishops, one must presume that deacons, too, were either chosen by the church or at least required the church's consent for their ordination. Yet the fact that only the local bishop touched them in the act of ordination indicates their special relation to the bishop. One might almost think of ancient deacons as extensions of their bishop. They carried out the practical details of church life, including administration of the treasury and distribution of welfare. The fact that the bishop alone ordained them, without participation of the other deacons in laying on hands, manifested that they were thought of less as an ongoing collegium in their own right than as extensions of the bishop. Their work was distinctive, but it must always proceed out of and minister to the unity of the congregation that was embodied in the bishop.

The oldest reference we have to bishops and deacons already pairs the two titles. It is found in the salutation of Paul's letter to the Philippians (1:1), and it antedates the creation of the "monarchic episcopate" by several decades. For Paul, the local "bishops" (*episkopoi*) were plural in number, and they may have been leaders of house churches.[11] There may have been an element of historical accident in the close relationship of the titles of bishops and deacons; it may simply have been the preferred nomenclature of some influential Pauline congregations. The close association of these titles, then, would not have arisen out of a deliberate decision to subordinate the church's active, practical administration sacramentally to the church's unity. The formula for ordinations worked out in the course of the second century, however, has precisely this close association as its point: the active life of the church is a function of its unity.

The presbyters, on the other hand, formed a limited exception to the rule of the centrality of the local bishop in ordaining. Hippolytus laid down the rule that the existing presbyters join in laying on hands at the ordination of a new presbyter. He then went on to claim that they were not really ordaining the new presbyter, since only the bishop ordains. They were merely "sealing" or confirming the bishop's action (*Apostolic Tradition* 8.1, 9.6–8). Hippolytus, himself a bishop and very anxious about the unity of the church (which he himself had breached at Rome), is not entirely persuasive on this point. If the bishop alone was ordaining the new presbyter, it is at least odd that the other presbyters participated with the same sacramental gesture that the bishop was using. Indeed, I suspect that the only reason Hippolytus denied that the presbyters were ordaining is that any ordinary observer would surely have drawn the conclusion that they *were* — and Hippolytus wanted to nip that quite obvious and defensible conclusion in the bud.

Here, as in the case of the diaconate, there may be historical reasons that helped define the relationship between bishop and presbyters. The New Testament evidence suggests that there may well have been a time when a college of presbyters was one fairly widespread option for local church governance, while bishops-with-deacons formed another. Only the relatively late Pastoral Epistles actually bring the two sets of terminology together; and they do it in a somewhat ambiguous way that may or may not suggest that bishops could be equated with presbyters. Yet they never associate deacons with presbyters in the way that they associate deacons with bishops.[12]

Perhaps the presbyterate was originally quite independent of the episcopate and was only subsequently brought into clear relationship with it. In that case, the second century will have seen the merging of two originally independent types of church organization. Elements of both would have been preserved in the forms of ordination. Bishops ordained deacons because they always had ordained them. Presbyters, however, joined the bishop in ordaining other presbyters because they had always been responsible for their own number. Ritual, after all, is notoriously conservative. Still, historical origins cannot tell us what meaning the rites had at the end of the second century any more than etymology can define the meaning of a word over its entire life span. What do the peculiarities of the ordination of presbyters tell us about the meaning of the presbyterate in the classic threefold model of ordination?

Despite Hippolytus's disclaimer, the rite tells us that presbyters do ordain presbyters, but only in conjunction with the bishop. It also tells us that the bishop ordains presbyters, but only in conjunction with the college of presbyters. This implies that the bishop and presbyters are closely associated, but that the presbyters cannot be, as it were, dissolved into the bishop in the way the deacons could be. The deacons are extensions of the bishop. The presbyters are, rather, a council of the community serving alongside the bishop. In order to avoid any suggestion that the community might have more than one center of unity, the presbyters do not add persons to their own number without the bishop's cooperation; yet they have an existence of their own, implying a direct sacramental relationship to the community that does not merely derive from the bishop.

In the ordinations of both deacons and presbyters, the leading role of the bishop in laying on hands embodies the connection with the church catholic. The life of the local church goes on in unity with the life of the larger church; and the ordained ministries, as sacramental reflections of that life, have to be tied into a wider network of ministry. The bishop is the officer who can express and maintain this in ordination because he or she embodies sacramentally the unity of the local church, both internally and with the church catholic.

The classic model of ordination created, through sacramental touching, a kind of network in which all the ordained participated. It was an "ecumenical" network in the ancient sense, that is, as nearly coterminous with the inhabited world as ancient Mediterranean people could imagine. It was catholic in the way it connected local churches with their contemporaries and with the church of the past. As early as the last decade of the first century,

church leaders were beginning to stress the continuity of authority within the church from the apostles on down. By the late
second century, mainstream Christians accepted the notion that
the classic formula for ordained ministry was in fact an apostolic
creation. While they seem to have been mistaken as to the actual
history, the ordination rites gained meaning from this belief and
offered a powerful image for understanding the life of the church
itself as a continuous fabric.

The classic rites of ordination, then, had this to say: the church
is a single, ecumenical community realized in local dioceses, but
bound together in catholic unity by its common derivation from
the apostolic preaching and by the holiness of the gospel communicated through that preaching. The ordained ministry existed
partly for functional reasons—to carry certain delegated bur-
dens of the church's daily life—but also partly to be a sacramental expression of the more diffuse truth about the church's
identity. Therefore, the rites of ordination expressed the *unity* of
the church by making the bishop the linchpin of the network.
The rites retained a sense of *catholic* diversity by bringing in
neighboring bishops to ordain the local bishop and by preserving
a somewhat independent identity, tradition, and tactile network
for the church's presbyters or elders. The church's *holiness* is
made sacramental in the connection between bishop and deacons, so that the image of daily service in an unclean world is
brought into the closest possible proximity with the center of
local church life. And the church's *apostolicity* is made sacramental in the network of ordinations itself: no one receives the message, the authority, the sacramental identity of ordained
ministry directly from God but rather from other persons, thus
being incorporated into a great chain of witnesses through whom
the gospel remains alive.

The sacramental touching incorporated in the laying on of
hands is therefore not a trivial aspect of the ordination rites. If we
focus on it to the exclusion of its proper context in the celebration
of word and sacrament, the election of the ordinands, and the
consent of the larger church, we may be tempted to offer magical
explanations of the act of touching. Some may even suggest that
an authority or power quite independent of the good news or of

the Christian community is being conveyed. Others may respond by questioning or rejecting the sacramental gesture that has been thus misrepresented. Neither of these misfortunes, however, is inevitable. The gesture of laying on hands in ordination is not magical, but sacramental. It embodies, on the sacramental level, diffuse but important realities of the church's life of faith. As such, it becomes a way for the church to speak of and represent its own life more clearly as life in the gospel of Jesus.

Chapter 5

Tactile Networks of Ordination

IN THE PRECEDING CHAPTER, I HAVE PRESENTED AN ANALYSIS OF the classic threefold ministry in historic succession, based on its sacramental relationship to the gospel and the community of the gospel. My goal, however, is not to justify the classic model over against others. I believe this line of approach can do something much more useful. It can help all of us appreciate the way all Christian traditions of ordination express the fundamental values and identity of their communities. I have not tried to show (nor do I think it possible or desirable to show) that the classic pattern is the only conceivable way of creating a sacrament of the church's life. It is enough that the classic pattern has been a longstanding fact of church life for most Christians, and that it embodies elements of the good news that stands at the heart of Christianity.

The recognition, however, that ordination is a kind of tactile, physical language, speaking sacramentally about the life of the church, reminds us that a language can utter more than one thing. The classic pattern is one possible discourse that can be framed in the language of orders. There are other possible discourses as well. We have already noted that at least two "patterns of speech" (presbyters, bishop-with-deacons) were available at the beginning of the second century, and that they were merged to form the classic pattern of orders. The fact that some diversity existed at the beginning means that Christians can never completely refuse to contemplate the possibility of diversity in subsequent ages. As in the second century, however, we must decide what we wish to say together in our common language.

Certainly, many discourses exist in the practice of ordination among Christians today.[1] The ancient formula continues in use among Anglicans, Roman Catholics, Old Catholics in communion

71

with Utrecht, some Lutherans, the Eastern Orthodox and other ancient Eastern churches, the united churches of the Indian subcontinent and Sri Lanka, the Philippine Independent Church, and a few other Christian communities. Among Protestant churches, a number of other patterns may be found. These include episcopal systems that are similar to the classic pattern but are not interconnected with the classic network of ordinations, presbyteral systems that acknowledge only one order of ordained ministry, and systems where ordination is performed primarily by laypersons as the congregation's acknowledgment that it recognizes a call to ministry and a *charisma* for it in the individual being ordained. In all of these and in their combinations and permutations, different specific statements are being made about the nature of the Christian communities that ordain and about their interconnections with or divergences from other Christian communities.

It is not my intention to explore or interpret any of these alternative patterns of ordination in the way that I have just done with the classic pattern. Indeed, I think it would be difficult for an outsider, lacking real familiarity with the tradition in question, to do so. Yet I think that the same kind of analysis I have applied to the classic model would prove instructive in each case. If we are to see how ordination might become a factor contributing to the unity of Christian people rather than inhibiting it, we need to think carefully about the kind of tactile networks that various ordination patterns set up and maintain and what these networks signify. What exactly are we saying through our various orders about the identity of our communities? What do we wish to begin saying as we reclaim our love for one another?

THE BISHOP'S AMBIGUOUS ROLE

First, we should take a brief step backwards to think over the ancient insistence that ordination be done by bishops only, whether acting by themselves in the case of deacons, or in concert with the local presbyterate in the case of presbyters, or in concert with episcopal colleagues in the case of other bishops. I believe that this insistence derived from the early Christians' pervasive (and justified) anxiety about the church's potential for fragmentation. This concern about unity marks the early epistolary literature from the New Testament onward and also the polemical literature "against heresies" that began to surface in the second century. Concern for unity gave rise to "rules of faith" and subsequently to creeds. It was the background against which the third-century church worked out its response to intensified persecution. And it put a deep imprint on the classic pattern of orders.

This concern for unity was not only practical but also deeply theological. The high-priestly prayer of Jesus, in John's account of the Last Supper (John 17), focuses above all on the goal of unity among Jesus' followers and between them and God. This is not a prayer about "church unity" in the modern sense, but about the mystical union of believers in and with God.[2] Still, it does seem to involve some kind of social unity as a consequence. If Christians are not on speaking terms with one another, and if they refuse to eat the sacred meal together but indulge in polemics against one another, it seems reasonable to conclude that they do not love one another. On the other hand, love does not necessarily imply merging church bureaucracies or setting uniform patterns for every aspect of church life. It sets up a standard not of uniformity but of genuine appreciation and reverence for one another in our diversity.

Paul speaks to this point in 1 Corinthians, a letter provoked in large part by the tendency of Corinthian Christians to form rival factions under the names of Paul, Apollos, or other esteemed Christian leaders. In combating this tendency, Paul says, among other things, "Do you not know that you are God's temple and the Spirit of God dwells in you? If anyone destroys God's temple, God will destroy this person. For God's temple is holy—and that is what you are" (1 Cor. 3:15–17). Because of subsequent revivals of purity thinking among Christians, we expect Paul to write that some kind of "abomination" (i.e., a purity violation) is threatening the holiness (purity) of the Christian community. Not so. The context makes it clear that the threat to holiness comes not from physical impurity, about which Paul cared relatively little, but from rivalries over leadership that resulted in the factionalizing of the community. Faction destroys the church's unity, and with it, its holiness. The gospel's innate tendency is toward overcoming barriers among human beings, not erecting new ones. The church's own tendency to divide appeared to undermine the gospel message.

Under the circumstances, it is not surprising that Christians moved, over a period of a century or so, to a self-contained system of ordinations in a practical effort to limit claims to leadership in the church and curb the resulting tendency to endless division. There were major losses in this process, since the early Christians adopted contemporary community standards for leadership that involved excluding women from public office. Their choices in this regard undoubtedly derived from their wish to create an impression of respectability in the environing society—a wish intimately linked to the growing anxiety about persecution. Yet in itself, the focus on unity, as I have already argued, was not only practical; it grew out of the good news itself.

The centrality of the bishop in ordination, then, was both a practical safeguard against schism and a sacramental realization of the church's unity. As such it contained potentially ambiguous messages. It expressed the gospel demand for love among the faithful and, indeed, among all human beings. It also expressed the church's insistence on its own practical unity. Much of the time these two may coexist; but it is always possible for the church to stray so far from the good news as to become, in effect, an enemy of the gospel. At such times the good news and the church's unity may no longer be mutually compatible. The church of the Inquisition was such a church; the church that justified chattel slavery and excluded people of color from ordination in the eighteenth and nineteenth centuries was such a church. Particularly important for the modern question of orders is the fact that, in the late Middle Ages, many of the faithful concluded that the church in the West had not only abandoned the gospel in favor of proclaiming itself and maintaining its own influence and wealth, but was even trying to prevent the gospel from being preached and heard.

In parts of Europe at the time of the Reformation, the bishop's role in ordaining became painfully ambivalent. While sacramentally the bishop continued to be a sign of the church's unity in love, in practice the bishop became a focus for all that was false and antigospel in the life of the church. Indeed, the bishop might sometimes be precisely the person who had most to lose in any effort to restore the primacy of the gospel and who would therefore resist it most strenuously. In such circumstances, the ancient rule that bishops are necessary for ordination might save the church from schism only at the cost of destroying the church's own true identity under the gospel.

The Church of England was not forced to choose between bishops and the gospel during the Reformation. Anglicans are in no position, however, to judge those who were. No decision of history can ever be adequately remade. If we who are at peace criticize those who opted, as they saw it, for the gospel under circumstances of great or even mortal danger, it may prove nothing more than shallowness on our part. The point, then, is not to remake historic decisions but to understand them and to sympathize with people who were seeking to be faithful under circumstances we may be thankful are not ours.[3]

We have the freedom to do this. The classic pattern of orders is not identical with the good news but a tertiary expression of it, emerging from the good news as it shapes the life of the church. This does not make it unimportant, but it does mean that it is something less than an absolute given. It is a meaningful sacrament of the church under the gospel, which we can seek to understand and appropriate under the gospel. It is not a purity code to be obeyed at all cost under threat of being cut off from God's presence if we fail. If what began as a defense against schism should become, under certain circumstances, a defense against the gospel itself, then it violates its own positive purpose and must, in those circumstances, be discarded.

HEARING WHAT ORDERS SAY

Even under the best of circumstances, the ancient rule about episcopal ordinations tells us much about preventing schism and little about repairing it. As a sacrament of the church's unity and love, the classic pattern of orders will have to undergo renewal before it can again be a commonly acknowledged and powerful safeguard of that unity. Because of the church's essential catholicity, we can rule out one solution to the problem of renewal from the start. No

solution that ignores the realities of the Reformation is adequate
to the task. The church cannot reclaim its catholicity while, at the
same time, ignoring a substantial portion of its own past. Any
future ecumenical pattern of orders must exhibit continuity both
with the classical model and with Protestant ministries of the
Reformation and thereafter.

Fortunately, we can at least begin to hear the multiple patterns
of orders characteristic of Christianity from the Reformation onward as varying expressions in a common language. This does not
mean they will be easy to reconcile. Not every utterance in a given
language, of course, agrees with every other utterance. The multiple patterns do, however, have a common syntax, so that all groups
who now wish to find a common utterance have the means to do so
at hand. We can analyze our present discourse in common terms.

How might this sort of analysis work?[4] As an example, I take
the Lutheran tradition in its German form, which, I gather, is
basically determinative of current usage among American Lutherans. What does this variety of orders "say"? How might it go on to
say something more ecumenical? In the Lutheran Reformation in
Germany, the tactile network of bishops was abandoned, but the
tactile network of presbyters (henceforward understood as a single order of ordained pastors) continued. The shift from the old
pattern—where the bishop had been essential to the ordination
even of a presbyter, to a new one in which the presbyteral college
could act on its own—meant making a break with one aspect of
the old network, but not with all aspects; for even in the classic
pattern, presbyters laid hands on presbyters.

The German Lutheran network (or "succession"), thus created, was expressing both continuity with the past and also a
break from it. Both of these expressions were theologically significant for Lutherans and therefore worth concretizing in the sacrament of ordination. The retention of presbyteral orders indicated
the Lutherans' unwillingness to think of themselves as departing
significantly from catholicity; the break with episcopal orders
expressed their unwillingness to set any tertiary Christian institution, however venerable, on a level with the gospel itself.[5] The
German Lutheran network of ordination was thus making a clear
and substantive statement about the nature of the particular

Christian community that was using these orders to form a sacrament of its own renewed life under the gospel.

I do not mean the preceding paragraphs as a historical statement about the intentions of the early Lutheran reformers, and I
would not be competent to make such a claim. I am only suggesting that the orders can be read in this way—and seem to be read in
much this way by American Lutherans today. One can therefore
hear these orders as speaking intentionally about a concern for
catholic continuity combined with an overarching concern to
maintain the priority of the gospel. On the other hand, the result
is a system of orders that is strictly Lutheran in a relatively limited
(and perhaps limiting) sense, embodying a particularly Lutheran
history. More "catholic" Christians might understandably see the
element of continuity here as being less powerful than the element
of discontinuity or even of separatism. The next question, then, is
whether Lutheran orders can or should begin to speak something
more broadly and ecumenically understandable even while they
continue to speak their existing message.

If Lutherans should wish to do so, one way to begin would be
to reclaim the order of bishops in the classic sense and reinstitute
the classic pattern of ordinations. This would indicate a serious
interest in reclaiming continuity with the majority of Christians
it seemed necessary to break at the Reformation. Yet there are
problems with such a proposal. The fundamental problem is that
such a move might be "heard" in several ways, some of which
would be illegitimate from a Lutheran perspective and also, I
think, ecumenically undesirable. Might the reclaiming of the
episcopate "in historic succession" be read as signifying an intention to undo or reverse the Reformation? This would scarcely be
desirable from an Anglican perspective since we, too, are a people of the Reformation. But beyond that, it would ultimately
mean a reduction of catholicity for the whole church of the future. Efforts to cancel the past lead only to confusion and impov-
erishment of identity. In any case, there is nowhere for Lutherans
to "go back" to. The church that Luther revolted against no
longer exists in any concrete sense. The Roman Church of today
is in some respects the same, but it is far from identical with the
Western Catholicism of the early sixteenth century. If Lutherans

tried to reverse their history by "going back" to the Roman Church, it would be a fantasy undertaking. The gospel is not about fantasy, but about real existence in this world.

On the other hand, a restoration of episcopate "in historic succession" could mean something quite different. It could be a way of affirming that the Reformation has by now succeeded—has gained its point about the priority of the good news. In that case, Lutherans could look for a way to bring their distinctive Reformation succession back into interconnection with the classic network of ordinations without submerging or negating either their history or their theological commitments. This could be done easily enough with proper precautions. Elements of the revised rite of ordination would make it clear that the college of presbyters claims the rite to ordain other presbyters on their own, if necessary in order to preserve an ordained ministry subordinate to the gospel, but that they normally ordain in the company and with the consent of the bishop as sacramental expression of the church's unity. This point could be made in several ways. A preface might state it verbally, with due acknowledgment of the bishop's role as sacrament of unity. Or the rite might have the presbyters invite the bishop to join them in the laying on of hands instead of merely gathering around the bishop as in the older tradition.

THE COMPLEXITY OF "CONNOTATIONS"

This is an oversimplified example, to be sure, of the way in which churches speak or might speak about their life through the rites of ordination. In reality, it is all a good deal more complicated. Experience in dialogue between American Episcopalians and Lutherans (both of the Evangelical Lutheran Church in America and of the Missouri Synod) has taught me that, in addition to the central issues, such as I have just raised, a host of other elements in a church's life becomes entangled in the discussion of orders. As with words, the resulting connotations may be as important to the meaning of the rite as its central "denotation." As a result, the ordained ministry of each church means something quite different to the church itself from what it means to its partner in dialogue, particularly in terms of connotations.

Take, for example, the episcopal succession in U.S. Anglicanism. What does it "say" to Episcopalians about their identity? It signifies a link to the whole broad extent of catholic Christianity and specifically to the ancient churches of the British Isles. It refers to the Reformation that renewed Anglicanism as well as to the many centuries of pre-Reformation church life. It has a specifically American significance, having been brought here after the Revolution at some sacrifice and at the initiative of American church leaders. It is embedded in a church life that places strong stress on representative institutions and the importance of the whole people of God; therefore it speaks to us of a church with bishops, not of bishops who rule, control, or otherwise stand over against the church.

For Americans of Lutheran persuasion, on the other hand, the Anglican episcopate in the United States often has overtones of foreignness (it is seen as English) and of aristocracy, if not autocracy (it seems to have an antidemocratic "feel" for them). It awakens associations with the pre-Reformation and Counter-Reformation episcopate of central Europe and has little association with the Reformation. It appears parochially Anglican rather than "catholic" in the expansive sense of the word. It may even seem to be antigospel, there being a persistent fear that Episcopalians, in ecumenical conversation, want Lutherans to "add" some separate and equal principle to the gospel by taking on the "historic episcopate," thereby making themselves truly pleasing to God.

Lutheran orders in the United States are equally ambiguous in terms of their connotations. American Lutherans are apt to hear their own networks of ordination as proclaiming the supremacy of the gospel. Their ordained ministries speak to them of a church life that is thoroughly American and democratic while also linked to European forerunners. While they acknowledge changes made at the time of the Reformation, their succession also speaks to them of continuity with earlier centuries of Christian life under the gospel. Their success over past decades at bringing together many different Lutheran traditions in the United States, some of them with rather different practices regarding ordination, speaks to them of the adaptability—perhaps even the relative insignificance—of the details of ordination as long as the gospel is kept in view.

For Episcopalians, Lutheran orders in the United States express some of these same things, but the evaluation of them is apt to shift a little. Where Lutherans may hear their orders speak of a limited discontinuity at the Reformation, Episcopalians may hear in them a major break, far more significant than our own. Episcopalians, having an ordained ministry that signifies continuity as much as reform, may find the message of the Lutheran successions one-sided. They may also hear Lutheran orders less in "American" terms than as defined by European ethnicities—much as Lutherans see Episcopalians! Some Episcopalians may also feel that Lutherans have their own "separate and equal" principle of ordained ministry to place alongside the gospel—that they treat Lutheran orders as de facto inalterable in any ecumenical context.

Each tradition is making statements about itself through its orders; but significantly, people of other traditions hear the statements differently from people of the "speaking" tradition. This is not surprising, since each group has its own history and will inevitably see others through the lenses of its peculiar experience. It requires a great leap of the imagination, prepared by careful study and prolonged inquiry, to begin seeing through another's eyes. And is that even the point? It is no doubt helpful, but it will not by itself alter the ecumenical situation. The real challenge is to find something we wish to say in common and the language to say it.

And here the problem runs still deeper, in the form of an anxiety not merely about our identity but about our *purity*. Each denomination believes itself to be pleasing to God at least partly by reason of its own purity. This is the way of human religion even among those who would reject it theologically. Any impurity might threaten our acceptability with God. Therefore the touch of less acceptable, less pure Christians threatens us profoundly. We believe that our own orders are essentially without fault, and therefore contact with those of our neighbors can only defile them. We fear contamination, impurity, loss of favor. When we talk about orders, we are always wrestling covertly with this issue of purity.

Often this leads us to want to return to the past and put it "right"—to say what went right here and what went wrong there, to apportion blame, to seek reparations for past injuries or errors. Eventually we hope to get everything "pure," to root out everything faulty. But that is, in fact, a hopeless procedure and only digs the trenches deeper. We wind up justifying our theological and ecclesiastical forebears and damning those of others (or, in more ecumenical circles, criticizing them politely without ever really entering into dialogue). The past created our present problems, however unintentionally. It will not resolve them. The only useful course of action is to examine our varying orders as they now are, with their full range of connotations, both for "speakers" and for "hearers." Then we can seek to determine how all that is positive (all that expresses the gospel) in each denomination's tradition can be preserved in a movement toward unity, and how all that is negative in our regard for one another can be obviated by overcoming the alienation that makes us impure to one another.

The question remains: What do we want to say together? The idea of replacing one succession by another is untenable because it would falsify the past and betray catholicity. The idea of moving toward unity while leaving ordination as it is, with no concrete points of interconnection among the varying networks, is equally untenable. How could diverse churches overcome their purity taboos against one another as long as the persons who are sacraments of the one church's life could not touch those of the other? The only ecumenical solution possible is to create networks that genuinely and deliberately incorporate the existing successions while, at the same time, look forward to a future church and ministry that will be fully and effectively catholic and apostolic, continuous with the entire Christian past and welcoming to all people of the present. Our orders must say yes to the churches we now are but, more importantly, yes to the church we might become.

A MODE OF ANALYSIS

If we wish to move in this direction, we must begin with a kind of "close reading" of our traditions of orders, a sustained and irenic effort to hear what they say. I have in mind an attentive and detailed reading, but not primarily a legal one. We should concentrate not on "why our orders are valid, efficacious, pure, etc., and yours are inadequate" or, in the more Protestant alternative, on "why ours are perfect and sufficient in their simplicity and yours are baroque and unnecessary." Instead, we should concentrate on "what we associate with our orders and with yours, and how the gospel does or does not enter into these associations." Our analysis should include the following:

1. the syntax of our speech—the details of the ordination networks themselves;
2. the mythos, or sacred stories, that each network evokes for us;
3. the theological points to which each alludes;
4. the practical needs and circumstances that have shaped them and continue to do so; and
5. the nature of the values we wish to maintain in and through them—gospel values, purity values, or whatever.

It will be impossible for one person, working out of one tradition, to do this kind of analysis effectively. It can be done only in ecumenical conversation, specifically in conversation dominated by the desire to create peace and unity rather than the desire to fight old wars and demonstrate the superiority of one's own tradition. (This may mean that it has to happen in informal, unofficial conversations, not in official ones.) What I can do here is to begin clarifying the categories of analysis I am suggesting.

Syntax

It is important to be clear about the pattern of orders normal to each tradition—not to construct an idealized form, but to know what is actually done. I do not mean to encourage the construction of artificial or legalistic models. If a particular tradition is, in fact, highly variable, that is important to know; it is part of the tradition's syntax. The point of this first step in analysis is to "read" the texts as literally as possible. Who lays hands on whom and to what express end? What is the subject of the sentence, the verb, the object, the objective complement?

Mythos

Are there stories that go along with each particular tradition of orders? At ordinations, Episcopalians like to think of their bishops' orders as reaching back somehow to remotest times. We may think of the old Celtic churches and of the mission of Augustine of Canterbury. We are likely to think of Samuel Seabury and his difficult quest to bring episcopal orders to North America, of William White and his role in supporting the Revolutionary cause, of Jackson Kemper and the then revolutionary idea of "missionary bishops," of significant figures in the earlier history of the local diocese. What associations do other churches make? What stories do they or might they tell in relation to ordination? How do these stories embody the meaning of their orders?

Theological Points

In some traditions, orders also evoke particular theological issues. These may become audible in the mythos, or perhaps they are better stated in more abstract forms. Does a given tradition of orders give utterance to a theological rationale? Did the tradition revise or shape its orders in accordance with the theological rationale? Or does the rationale postdate the orders? What is the rationale? How is it heard as relating to the central issues of faith in the gospel? Much of this book is devoted to answering questions of this sort for the Anglican tradition. On the whole, this is probably the most thoroughly examined aspect of orders. Yet our theological associations can lead us astray if allowed to capture our attention prematurely. Orders are normally prior to or, at least, more fundamental then their verbal explication in theology.

Practical Needs

To what extent have immediate practical needs of the past or present shaped a given tradition of orders? For example, how did African-American churches respond to the need for ordained ministry in a climate of church and society that tended to dismiss their people as unfit for ordination? When Episcopalians commemorate Absolam Jones, we find we must both celebrate his ordination and repent of the slowness and reluctance of the Anglo-American church authorities in the matter. Other African-Americans dealt with the same practical problems differently. How they did is a part of what the orders of predominantly African-American churches mean today. Like the theological points, these practical issues, particularly where they determined important contingent, historical choices, will often emerge in the mythos. There is also an ongoing dialectic between orders and the practical functions of the ordained in the church—a dialectic that (sometimes subtly) affects our sense of the meaning of orders. There is no wall separating the rites by which a person is ordained and the use to which the church then puts that person. The interaction between the two is powerful enough to warrant examination in its own right. How, for example, does the work that a deacon does interact with the way in which a deacon is ordained?

Values

Finally, when we understand as clearly as possible *what* our various orders are saying, we must think about the values implicit in those messages. Since the church militant is never sinless, faultless, or inerrant, we must expect to find that all of us hold mixed values, some of them deriving from the good news of Jesus, others from quite opposite sources—legalism, self-seeking, hypocrisy, anxieties about purity, and the desire to establish our own superiority in God's eyes. If we want to be people of the gospel, we may have to abandon some values we have treasured in the past. If we can agree to treasure the gospel above all else, we shall increasingly, I believe, find ourselves on the path to loving unity.

What I am urging here is a kind of conversation among Christians that is devoted not to showing who is right about orders and who is wrong, but to listening as our orders speak, first in a common tongue, and finally I hope, with a common discourse. Genuine conversation cannot occur without mutual respect and affection—not too much to ask, as they are basic elements in

Christian love. We all need to become more conscious of what we are saying, how it is being heard, what others are saying, how we have been mistaking their meaning, and what values we hold in common as people of the gospel. This kind of conversation is not, of course, limited to the arena of orders, but it will do little good to hold it in other areas of our life if we ignore this one. For our orders are talking all the time—less vocally, but often more persuasively than our words.

Chapter 6

Toward a Sacramental Realization
of the Church's Unity

FULL COMMUNION

WE CAN AGREE IN PRINCIPLE THAT CHRIST BESTOWED UNITY ON the church, a unity that Christians are now seeking to understand and reclaim. It is less easy to agree about what that unity ought to look like at the end of the second millennium. In earlier ages, it has taken a variety of forms and has seldom, if ever, existed in perfect realization. From earliest times, there were divisions among Christians. Sometimes wise and temperate action, as in the appointing of the Board of Seven (Acts 6:1–7), averted schism. At other times, truly fundamental differences of belief, as in the Gnostic controversies of the second century, made division inevitable.

In the pre-Constantinian era, the unity of the church consisted primarily in maintaining intercommunication among congregations, with mutual respect and deference. There was no juridical unity or centralization—indeed, no way for such a thing to exist in the Roman Empire without imperial patronage. Only in individual provinces, such as Egypt or Africa, was there a degree of organizational coherence expressed, beginning in the third century, in the gathering of councils of bishops (as in the province of Africa) or in certain rights of primacy belonging to the bishop of the principal city (as in Egypt). In times of major perplexity, the churches of a minor province might appeal for guidance to the bishop of a major center. In times of perceived danger to the unity of the church, the bishop of a major center might seek to interfere in the affairs of a congregation at a distance. On the whole, the church's organizational pattern in the second and third centuries was loose—more nearly a network than a fixed structure.

After the imperial family adopted Christianity as its religion, the old ways no longer seemed adequate. Constantine encouraged a large-scale conciliar system, which was a kind of development and codification of the older episcopal networks. The councils, in turn, fostered the growth and regularization of the metropolitical system, a graded hierarchy among bishops culminating in the patriarchal sees of Aelia (Jerusalem), Alexandria, Antioch, Constantinople, and Rome. The whole system came more and more to resemble the empire's political structure.

Subsequently, these great sees pulled away from each other as each struggled for dominance. In the East, this culminated in divisions over Christology, which split Alexandria, Antioch, and Jerusalem from Constantinople. Between Constantinople and Rome, a prolonged dispute over precedence and other issues finally produced a long lasting division. Subsequently, many of these territorially defined jurisdictions were further fragmented in conflicts over status and doctrine. In the East, Constantinople gave up parts of its jurisdiction to the new patriarchate of Moscow and to various autocephalous churches, but retained communion with them. In the West, the Reformation not only challenged the Roman pontiff's jurisdiction but launched a process of disintegration that divided Protestants from one another as well as from the Church of Rome.

The greater fragmentation of Western Christianity may partly reflect the greater political security of the West during the modern era; Christians dominated by a Moslem empire or struggling to achieve nationhood under adverse circumstances probably had less leisure for internal fighting. On the other hand, a particular kind of organizational rigidity, characteristic of our tradition, may also have been a factor in what happened to Western Christianity. The focusing of the unity of the Western church upon a single bishop (and thus, inevitably, upon a single court bureaucracy) had proved helpful while the church was fighting for independence from feudal authorities. It later proved counterproductive for dealing with doctrinal issues, since structural uniformity was increasingly incapable of coexisting with meaningful diversity of thought.

The church of the late twentieth century, if it seeks a renewal of unity, must learn how to handle diversity in ways more like those of the second and third centuries than those of the fifteenth. I am not suggesting that we automatically welcome or embrace all varieties of opinion claiming to be Christian. There are situations where that is impossible. Gnostic antagonism toward the material order, for example, is no more compatible with orthodox Christianity today than it was eighteen hundred years ago. I do mean to say, however, that we must learn how to agree about what is central, about the good news itself, and allow a broad openness about all subordinate questions. We must prize both unity and diversity.

Our unity lies in the gospel itself. In matters of interpretation, we must be prepared to tolerate, welcome, and, at times, endure a great deal of pluralism. This will be possible only as the grace of God in forgiving each of us eventuates in love for one another. As support for a common life of affirmation, acceptance, and love, the uniting church requires some institutional bonds of unity that will point in the direction Jesus has already pointed. They must be bonds significant enough to discourage people from hastily rejecting communion with one another, and also loose enough to keep those who are excessively confident of knowing the mind of God from politically dominating their more modest neighbors.

The most useful model for our times is probably not that of a centralized bureaucracy. Even if we discount the record of abuses against truth and charity that have accompanied such models in the past, excessive centralization simply does not respond well to the needs of an era demanding creativity. We have seen striking examples of this fact in the debacle of heavily centralized economies at the end of the 1980s. The principle is equally true in the church. Today Christianity is becoming indigenized throughout the world in cultures where it never struck deep root before, and is also struggling to understand and proclaim the gospel amidst major cultural shifts in the West. In such a time, it would be risky in the extreme for local churches to hand over too much authority to small, centralized groups of leaders who would, by the very nature of their employment, be talking mainly to one another. What is required is not centralized uniformity, but a strong commitment to a shared life marked by consultation and deference and carried out in love.

In the specific language that has become standard within Anglican circles, the renewal of the church's unity will take the form of "full communion" more than of "organic unity." Churches in full communion with one another place no barriers to the movement of the laity between them and recognize the full interchangeability of their ordained ministers, even though actual transfer of clergy between the churches is governed by normal canonical or procedural limitations. Such churches make a commitment to consult with one another. Even when they disagree about difficult issues, they will not quickly or lightly break communion, but will remain in association while they take every opportunity to hear and understand positions that may at first sound new or foreign to them. The churches retain their own existing identities and are independent in terms of internal organization, but they see themselves in a new and different context. They now know themselves to be actively part of a larger Christian community, and they behave accordingly.

TWO DESIDERATA

How existing church communities move toward full communion is a matter touching many aspects of their lives. It can be worked out only on a case by case basis. Above all, it depends on increasing our mutual trust of one another (and behaving in a way worthy of such trust) and on creating means of consultation among the churches. The central issues, however, are probably the sacramental ones. When we recognize the two great sacraments in one another's churches, we are acknowledging the presence of Christ there. When we find ways to create a ministry genuinely mutual to more than one church tradition, we are sacramentally declaring that we again understand ourselves as one.

How, then, can the churches, as they move toward renewal of unity, speak, in ordination, things continuous with their various histories and yet also open to a wider comprehension of Christian communion? Two things are necessary. First, we must learn how to speak all our historic ministries at once without canceling, breaking off, or merely submerging any one of them. Second, we must nonetheless agree on a single "sentence" that we want to speak together—a sentence rich in nuance, inclusive as the gospel is inclusive, and representing the re-initiation of genuinely common life rather than the capitulation of one tradition to another.

These two desiderata may appear to be in conflict with one another, but they are so only if we begin from a presupposition that is in fact contrary to the gospel. If we treat ordination as an act subject to purity codes, we shall be forever anxious lest an unclean person touch one of our own and render that person impure. Those of presbyterian convictions will be anxious about the contamination that a bishop's touch might bring. Those of episcopalian convictions will be anxious that the touch of a minister from a nonepiscopal tradition or of a bishop of alien succession may pollute or even invalidate the ordination of our own. These anxieties are not worthy of Christians. The gospel absolves us of them; for "everything God has created is good and nothing to be rejected if received with thanksgiving, for it is hallowed through God's word and prayer" (1 Tim. 4:3–4). This assurance frees us to take our own tradition and those of others seriously.

PRESERVATION OF EXISTING ORDERS

In order to attain our first desideratum—to learn how to speak all our historic ministries at once without canceling, breaking off, or contradicting any one of them—one thing is necessary, namely, that the minimum positive requirements of ordination in each tradition should continue to be met. We shall probably find general agreement that these requirements include presentation of the candidate by the church community and the laying on of hands with prayer by those authorized by the community to do so. As long as the prescribed persons continue to lay hands on those being ordained, there will be no reason to suppose that the community means to reject or cancel anything in its tradition of ordination. It does not—and, for the sake of the catholicity of the church, should not—cut itself off from its past. Our common purpose is to move on from the past, not to abandon it.

Our modern difficulties arise less from the positive requirements of any church than from the negative limitations that
churches sometimes place on the act of ordination—limitations
that serve primarily to question the authenticity of or reject communion with other churches. There can be no progress toward
unity without giving up these restrictions. I do not mean that
every restriction (for example, on who ordains) must disappear.
Some restrictions exist in order to give shape and reality to our
sacramental "words." Each Christian tradition chooses, for the
role of laying on hands, those whose participation enables the
church to say what it wishes to say positively about itself through
ordination. In the classic pattern of ordination, for example, only
persons already ordained as bishops or presbyters laid on hands.
This restriction was not primarily negative, since it was not created to deny the importance of others in the process of ordaining.
The ordination remained an act of the entire community, working
through those whom it had already clothed with certain sacramental meanings referring to the local community's relationship with
the church catholic.

The modern difficulties arise from rules of ordination that emphasize precisely the distance and even the lapse of communion
between one church and another. Anglicanism, for example, preserved the classic pattern from an earlier, pre-Reformation era
when the "message" of these orders was not primarily polemical.
Yet our understanding of our own orders did not emerge unscathed
from the era of conflict with Presbyterian, Congregationalist, or
Wesleyan dissidents. For many of us, the historic episcopate became
a sign of our distinctiveness and superiority vis-à-vis other Protestants. The successions of others were labeled "defective" or
"invalid," and therefore posed a threat of contamination if mingled
with our own. This kind of negative restriction must disappear if
Anglicans are to move toward an ecumenical unity.

Many modern Anglicans would feel some anxiety if a United
Methodist bishop joined in laying on hands at the ordination of a
bishop in the Episcopal Church. As long as the two churches are
not in communion, some sense of awkwardness is probably appropriate, for the act would speak sacramentally of a unity that has no
other concrete existence. Yet if the two churches move toward full

communion, it will become an appropriate act. The Episcopal Church would maintain its positive requirements, continuing to have the classic minimum of three co-consecrators representing our own episcopal succession; but it would drop negative provisions of its rites designed primarily to keep other church traditions at a distance. We would accept the gift of United Methodist orders as a movement toward ecumenical unity, as they would accept ours.

By preserving its minimal positive requirements, each church tradition makes clear its continuity with its past. By including the succession of other churches along with its own as it moves toward full communion with them, it looks toward a future of greater unity for the church at large. In each case, we shall have to drop the purity reaction that holds that "our" succession is pure and that of "the others" will contaminate it. This may be as big a problem for United Methodists in my hypothetical proposal as for Episcopalians, since each may see their own orders as coming under question or being diluted. In Christ, however, contamination no longer threatens us. We are not at risk of losing anything. Instead, we can rely on each succession remaining alive in communion with the other. Eventually, by participation of each church in the other's ordinations, the two successions or networks of ordination would be inextricably intertwined with each other, though they would continue to have distinct identities as long as the two separate church communities could be identified as distinct.

SPEAKING UNITY

But what of our second desideratum: that the churches agree on a single "sentence" that we can speak together—a sentence rich in nuance, inclusive as the gospel is inclusive, and representing a renewal of genuinely common life rather than the capitulation of one tradition to another? Can this desideratum be reconciled to the first? If each tradition retains its own continuity, how can they all speak the same thing? The history of the origins, codification, and maintenance of our traditions over the centuries is in large part a sad story of polemics against those different from us. How can we remain who we are and also renew our unity when our disunity is part of who we are?

It may be tempting to suggest that each tradition reserve ordination as something characteristic of Christian diversity more than of Christian unity. Perhaps it is enough in the modern world to express our agreement in written documents, mutual hospitality, and commitments for consultation and aid. The ordained ministries of the various churches could then be a matter purely for internal concern and regulation, of no real ecumenical importance. The difficulty with such a suggestion is that ordination is one of the most powerful (because sacramental rather than verbal) ways in which a church speaks of its own identity. If our orders go on speaking something diametrically opposite to our expressed intention for unity, they are likely to give disunity the last word.

There is a double danger, in fact. Refusal to unite ministries suggests a certain insincerity in our ecumenical intentions themselves. As long as the distinctiveness of each succession or network is jealously guarded and preserved, we shall be designating our distinctiveness as our most prized reality. What is more, failure to unite ministries creates a serious social threat to whatever unity we do achieve. Each church would continue to harbor an enormously influential subgroup (indeed, in the modern West, most of our professional leadership) defined in such a way as to make them centers of differentiation rather than of unity. Both the self-understanding and the self-interest of the ordained would emphasize their distinctiveness from their counterparts in the other churches. Full communion among churches without full interchangeability of ordained ministers would be only a phantom, destined to disintegrate at the first serious challenge.

GETTING FROM HERE TO THERE: THE HISTORIC EPISCOPATE

How, then, to proceed? We cannot start anew, as if there were no past to consider. Neither can we simply erase all of the polemics that have codified and confirmed our suspicions of one another. Of particular difficulty is the gap between traditions having bishops and those that not only do not have them, but have actively rejected the episcopal office. Two things must be said as a basis for working on this problem: one is that networks of ordination can only come together in *persons*, since persons are the nodes of such networks, and the bishop has traditionally been the person who has served this function; the second is that a bishop, in the terms I am using here, is to be defined sacramentally, not functionally. Each of these points requires some elaboration and clarification.

1. Ordination makes ordained persons sacraments of the church's life. As a sacramental act, it confronts us with all of the inconveniences and perplexities as well as the particular riches of concrete existence in time and space. It is one thing to declare that two Christian groups are in principle at one with one another; it is another thing to give that declaration concrete life. If orders are to make sacraments of the restoration of the church's unity, it can only be in the form of specific ordained persons whose ordination reflects this renewed reality. I have suggested how ordination can do this in the case of two churches that already have bishops (Episcopalians and United Methodists). But must it be done through bishops? Why not through presbyters or deacons or pastors or elders or whatever order happens to dominate the tradition of a given church?

The basic reason is simply that the episcopate is already "set up" for this purpose, defined for it by rites made to achieve this very end. The interaction of local and more ecumenical elements, both in the making of a bishop and in the bishop's own acts of ordination, designate the bishop as such. If we want another "office" to embody the same purpose, we shall have to set it up in imitation of the episcopate. It will simply be an episcopate under another name. This would be confusing, and not just for those churches that already have episcopates. If we create a completely new office, make an entirely new beginning, then none of us will know where we are in relationship to the past. By making a barrier against the past, we would make a barrier to catholicity rather than an opening toward it.

On the other hand, if the episcopal "meaning" were explicitly incorporated into the presbyterate or pastorate through changes in their rites of ordination, what would become of their existing sacramental meaning, that is, of the themes in the life of the church presently more closely associated with them? What be-comes, in the Reformed tradition, of the emphasis on the local presbytery? What becomes, in the Lutheran tradition, of the em-phasis on ministry of word and sacraments? These would not, of course, be abandoned, but neither would they survive unaltered or unimpaired. A "word" that means too many things may mean none of them very clearly.

It may be answered that the ecumenical aspect of orders is al-ready a collective responsibility of the presbyterate in Reformed churches or of the pastors in many Lutheran churches. That is un-doubtedly true. But how well does a collective body (which often does not really function effectively as such) serve as a *sacrament* of unity? In a presbytery, one is already dealing with a network. Con-ceptually, a network might serve as a node in a larger network, but it is not the easiest thing to grasp with the imagination. And sacra-ments must speak to the imagination. A single individual can provide a clear and distinct sacrament of the point of interconnec-tion between local and more comprehensive networks.

The value of the classic pattern of ordinations depends not merely on its being the oldest truly ecumenical pattern for them, or on its virtually exclusive predominance over most of Christian history, or on its continued use in modern churches containing a majority of living Christians. All of these are powerful induce-ments to consider it as an important option. They have had a powerful effect on ecumenical thinking. Yet they could still be seen as implying the capitulation of nonepiscopal traditions to episcopal ones. Thus they cannot be decisive ecumenical argu-ments for universal adoption of the episcopate. For the purposes of creating a network, however, which can convey, communicate, and maintain all the existing networks of ordination in a clear context of catholic unity, there appears to be no substitute for an episcopate, even if it is not called by that name.

2. We are speaking, however, of the sacramental aspects of the episcopate, not of its practical functions. As the Chicago-Lambeth Quadrilateral implies, Anglicans are not committed to any one method of organizing church life. Nor does church history suggest that bishops can be understood or utilized in only one way. The prince-bishop of late medieval Germany is neither an edifying nor

a necessary variant. The authority assigned to bishops is determined by the church itself in a given place and time. At one extreme stand certain modern bishops in the Roman Catholic or United Methodist churches who have sweeping powers over the clergy and property of their jurisdictions. At the other extreme one might locate the Irish-Scottish church of the early Middle Ages, which expected of bishops only that they lead lives of exemplary holiness and perform ordinations when called upon; effective authority over the church lay in the hands of the great abbots who were usually presbyters.

Most bishops in most ages have probably functioned in some kind of middle ground, limited by the rights, duties, and prerogatives of others in the church but possessing a substantial amount of influence or outright power. The bishop's sacramental role does not predetermine all functional arrangements. One could easily imagine a bishop who functioned as a presbyter among presbyters, though with special ecumenical responsibilities, and who was distinguished mainly by a focal role in ordaining and by the particular form of his or her own ordination. That would be sufficient to achieve the needed sacramental emphasis on the unity of the church. In some ways, it might even enhance the sacramental character of the episcopate, which would be identified clearly with unity, not with jurisdictional authority.

There would be no need for a church of, say, the Reformed tradition to break sharply with its own traditions of polity in order to accommodate such a person among its ordained ministers. Such a bishop would no more ordain without the rest of the presbytery than the rest of the presbytery would ordain without the bishop. In making such an adaptation, Reformed churches would be reasserting an aspect of the classic pattern sometimes neglected by episcopal churches. Even in churches where it is traditional for nonordained persons to join in laying on hands, reintroducing the sacramental role of the bishop need not preclude this practice; the bishop's participation would simply focus the ecumenical element in the ordination while the "local" element would continue to be expressed as before.

What I am urging, then, is an episcopate that exists primarily as the *sacramental* way of speaking the ecumenical unity of the church in the local context. The bishop embodies ecumenicity by virtue of the specific rite of episcopal ordination and conveys this element by a prominent role in local ordinations, ensuring that the ordained ministry is thus a sacramental realization of the life of the church catholic as well as of the local church. How the bishop figures in the practical details of church life and administration is a functional issue to be sorted out in accordance with local needs and traditions. The bishop may have extensive constitutional powers or only the moral weight inevitably accruing to the person who represents our Christian unity in the local congregation.

The point is not to effect a change in existing polities, far less to persuade the heirs of one polity to capitulate to those of another. The point is to ensure that ecumenicity figures in all of our orders in a prominent and recognizably common way—to ensure that the renewal of church unity is embodied in the sacramental language that tells us who we are as Christian communities. To do so, this unity must be incorporated in the image of specific persons whose role and meaning as sacraments is defined in the manner of their ordination. Since from the beginning, the historic episcopate has served precisely this purpose, we shall either have to make use of it creatively or try to reinvent it under some other name.

All bishops stand in a succession, that is, a network of touch such as characterizes all models of ordination. In the renewal of the church's unity, the "historic succession" of which the Chicago-Lambeth Quadrilateral speaks will be present alongside and in union with successions of other origin. All will meet and be united sacramentally in the persons of the bishops themselves. This mingling will extend rather than diminish the catholicity of all ordained ministers affected by it, sacramentally representing in them the restored and enhanced catholicity of the church itself. Our lingering dependence on purity codes will cause all or most of us to shrink from such a process at times. But the good news of Jesus is that God does not care for purity codes, and that we are free to act without fear on behalf of loving unity.

Conclusion

ORDERS HAVE BEEN A PROBLEM FOR THE ECUMENICAL MOVEMENT. They provide a powerful symbol of the present disunity of Christians. Presumably they could become again, as in antiquity, a powerful symbol of our unity. Getting from here to there, however, is a major challenge. In the preceding pages, I have sought to find a path by understanding ordination as a sacramental language and by hazarding at least the beginnings of a close reading of what Christians are saying through that language. We need a shared understanding of ordained ministry as a sacrament of the church's life and a willingness to frame ordination rites for the future that will honor, in their particulars, the history and the positive commitments of all churches. Given these, I believe that our present churches can journey toward a renewal of ecumenical unity.

This cannot happen, however, without our agreeing to say some new things together. Old patterns alone, even the most venerable of them, will not save us. The "episcopate in historic succession" was originally created more to prevent schism than to heal it. It cannot participate in the process of healing without acknowledging that, whatever misfortunes past schisms may have occasioned, all Christians are now faced with the need to reclaim communion with one another in order to restore the catholicity of the church and renew its unity. Other successions that have arisen among Protestant churches, either from historical necessity or in order to make a certain theological point, will also have to give up their claims to universal sufficiency. All of us alike will have to surrender our longstanding use of ministry as a sacrament of disunity.

People of all churches will find it necessary to shed anxieties about purity in order to allow the intermingling of our ministerial successions to create a new and more comprehensive network of ordinations. The gospel stands against purity codes. Purity codes are designed to shut the religiously less privileged out, but the gospel aims to bring them in. It is a perennial problem for Christianity that Christians are forever reinstating old and broken purity codes or devising new ones to take their place. We are not comfortable basing all our claim before God on God's grace; we want to have purity codes that will enable us to show our superiority over other human beings. The churches have long used the ministry as a particularly fruitful opportunity for constructing purity codes. Christian unity will be possible only as we desist and trust the good news of Jesus instead.

The primacy of the gospel relativizes all of our concern about the shaping of ordination or ordained ministry, but it does not invalidate it. The specifics of ordination are indeed worthy of careful consideration because they form a kind of language in which churches speak of their identity under the gospel. Through ordinations, we tell who we are, to whom we are joined, and from whom we are sundered. We evoke some things about the tradition of the local church, and we tell how the local church is connected to the church catholic. As the church's unity reemerges in the coming century, we shall require ordination rites that will make clear connections with the past while, at the same time, bridging the gaps among us in the present. Only so can we create a network of ordination that can serve as a sacrament of the church's life in the future.

It will not surprise anyone that an Anglican should argue for the historic episcopate as critical to this process of development. I hope, however, that the argument developed here is more than special pleading. It represents an effort to understand the situation from a position that is rooted in the Anglican tradition without regarding it as inherently superior to or purer than others. I have implied no doubts about the "validity" of other kinds of ordained ministries and can see no basis for such doubts. I have argued only that bishops in historic succession form the most suitable points of articulation between the local church and the larger network of ordinations—present, past, and future.

The goal of ecumenical unity requires a network of ordinations using bishops in the classic manner, but also deliberately

and expressly preserving all of our existing ministerial successions. In such a network, we shall be speaking sacramentally both
our past, with its divisions, and a present in which unity is being
reclaimed as our divine birthright. The resulting commingled succession will serve the future as a kind of sacramental recapitula-
tion both of the griefs of the past and of God's grace in
overcoming them. As such, it may even come to seem a succession
preferable to all of its predecessors because it is richer in testi-
mony to God's goodness to us.

Notes

Introduction

1. Much has been made of the differences, of course, particularly since the nineteenth century. Cf. Paul Bradshaw, *The Anglican Ordinal: Its History and Development from the Reformation to the Present Day* (London: SPCK, 1971), 128–57. None of the fine distinctions involved, however, would have had any point were not the two traditions very closely related indeed.

Chapter 1

1. I quote from the form given the Quadrilateral at the Lambeth Conference of 1888, the text given in the 1979 *Book of Common Prayer* of the Episcopal Church, 877.
2. Paul Bradshaw, *The Anglican Ordinal: Its History and Development from the Reformation to the Present Day* (London: SPCK, 1971), 172–208; Mary Tanner, "The Ecumenical Future," in *The Study of Anglicanism*, ed. Stephen Sykes and John Booty (London: SPCK; Philadelphia: Fortress Press, 1988), 379–93.
3. Quotations from the "Articles of Religion," 1979 *Book of Common Prayer* of the Episcopal Church, 867–76.
4. Richard A. Norris, "Episcopacy," in *The Study of Anglicanism*, 304–5. Cf. in the same volume the articles on "Ordinals" by Paul F. Bradshaw, 151–52, and "Ministry and Priesthood" by John B. Webster, 288–92.
5. It was recognized that under unusual circumstances laypersons could legitimately perform baptism.
6. Faith and Order Paper No. 111 (Geneva: World Council of Churches, 1982).
7. L. Wm. Countryman, *Dirt, Greed, and Sex: Sexual Ethics in the New Testament and Their Implications for Today* (Philadelphia: Fortress Press, 1988), 11–143.
8. See Paul's own summary in Rom. 14:1–15:21.

Chapter 2

1. So, for example, with John the Baptist or in the case of the strange exorcist of Luke 9:49–50.
2. L. Wm. Countryman, *Biblical Authority or Biblical Tyranny? Scripture and the Christian Pilgrimage* (Philadelphia: Fortress Press, 1981), 68–75.

3. I originally sketched out the ideas of the following argument in "The Gospel and the Institutions of the Church with Particular Reference to the Historic Episcopate," *Anglican Theological Review* 66 (1984): 402–15.

4. Cf. Frank Hawkins, "Orders and Ordination in the New Testament" and "The Tradition of Ordination in the Second Century to the Time of Hippolytus" in *The Study of Liturgy,* ed. Cheslyn Jones, Geoffrey Wainwright, and Edward Yarnold (New York: Oxford University Press, 1978), 290–306.

5. The importance of due succession also seems to be implied in the Pastoral Epistles (1 and 2 Timothy, Titus), though the term itself is not used. There is an excellent chance, however, that they were written after *1 Clement.*

6. Article XXV includes Orders in the group of "five commonly called Sacraments," but goes on to say that they are not "Sacraments of the Gospel." "An Outline of the Faith," which is the Catechism of the *Book of Common Prayer* currently authorized in the Episcopal Church in the United States, refers to ordination as one of the "other sacramental rites evolved in the Church under the guidance of the Holy Spirit." These rites are distinguished by the fact that "they are not necessary for all persons in the same way that Baptism and the Eucharist are."

7. The giving of the Spirit, not the words of Jesus, is the specific evidence cited by Peter to justify his action in baptizing the household of Cornelius: "So, if God had given them the very same gift as was given us when we believed on the Lord Jesus Christ, who was I to be able to stand in God's way?" (Acts 11:17).

8. The early second-century church order called the *Didache* shows that a similar state of affairs prevailed in some places for more than a generation after Paul's time. See the good sketch of New Testament usage in Kevin Giles, *Patterns of Ministry Among the First Christians* (Melbourne: Collins Dove, 1989), 151–69.

9. My exposition of the four notes of the church here may seem somewhat different from the usual. If so, that is because I am concerned to show them as consequences of the good news and not as independent principles in their own right. The more independent they are, the less weight can be given them.

10. I owe a special, if somewhat distant, debt to two books that launched my thinking on this topic many years ago: Arthur Michael Ramsey, *The Gospel and the Catholic Church,* new impression (London: Longmans, 1956), and A. G. Hebert, *Apostle and Bishop: A Study of the Gospel, the Ministry and the Church-Community* (New York: Seabury Press, 1963).

Chapter 3

1. The one exception seems to be the sacrament of absolution or reconciliation. But Luther was surely correct in seeing this practice as an extension of baptism rather than a separate and independent sacrament.

2. There is an analogy here with "performative utterance"—statements such as "By the authority vested in me, I hereby declare you to be a

graduate of this institution." These, however, are a rather limited and exceptional category of verbal language and seem often to require some physical token to give them force, such as the granting of a diploma.

3. Article XXVIII; cf. E. J. Bicknell, *A Theological Introduction to the Thirty-Nine Articles of the Church of England,* 3d ed. rev. by H. J. Carpenter (London: Longmans, 1955), 396–99.

4. *Apostolic Tradition* 1–9; I have used the translation of Burton Scott Easton (Cambridge: Cambridge University Press, 1934; repr. ed., Archon Books, 1962). The same pattern is found in *Apostolic Constitutions* 8.4–19.

5. Eusebius, *Church History* 6.29.

6. Hippolytus, however, requires even a confessor to be ordained in order to enter the episcopate (*Apostolic Tradition* 10). Since the bishop was the focus of unity in the local congregation and there was no other way to supply that focus, he had to be ordained to express the congregation's assent and its preparedness to obey and remain in communion with him, and also to express the consent of the surrounding churches. A presbyter, on the other hand, functioned as part of a collegium, and his status with the congregation was guaranteed by membership in that.

7. This is the practice assumed for presbyters in *Apostolic Constitutions* 8.16.4.

Chapter 4

1. One could even speak of "filling the hands of the altar," Ezek. 43:26.

2. For a fuller treatment of the topic of purity in ancient Israel and early Christianity, see L. Wm. Countryman, *Dirt, Greed, and Sex: Sexual Ethics in the New Testament and Their Implications for Today* (Philadelphia: Fortress Press, 1988), 11–143.

3. It remains ambiguous whether the daughter of Jairus was actually dead; but the same point is made in Luke 7:14, where he touches the bier on which the son of the widow of Nain lay. The bier would have been nearly as contagious of impurity as the corpse itself.

4. Heb. 6:1–2, by juxtaposing "teaching about washings" with "laying on of hands" and "resurrection of the dead," seems to confirm this association between baptism and laying on of hands, especially since it categorizes all of these as a "foundation" and as "the discourse of the beginning of Christ"—that is, as catechetical issues.

5. Kevin Giles, *Patterns of Ministry Among the First Christians* (Melbourne: Collins Dove, 1989), 184–88.

6. There may have been a connection with the Jewish practice of ordaining elders, but it remains uncertain; cf. Giles, *Patterns of Ministry,* 193–94.

7. "To lay hands on" someone is ambiguous in English, but not in Greek. The verb here is *epitithemi,* which is used to indicate the gesture of laying a hand peaceably on another person. When one wanted to indicate a violent use of the hands, the verb was *epiballo.*

8. Giles, *Patterns of Ministry,* 189–92, reads both passages as consistent with the earlier usage. He seems, however, to assume that Paul is the

actual author of the Pastorals. If, with most students of the subject, we date the letters in the second century, we can read them more literally and need not be surprised by the presence of actual ordination language in 2 Timothy.

9. E.g., *Philadelphians* 7.2; *Trallians* 2.2; *Magnesians* 7.1 (". . . and the presbyters"); cf. *Ephesians* 4.1, 20.2; *Magnesians* 4.1, 6.1–2; etc.

10. The development of the episcopate seems to have gone hand in hand with the progressive exclusion of women from community leadership. There does not seem, however, to have been any necessary, intrinsic relationship between the two developments. The exclusion of women was a concession to contemporary community standards, no longer justifiable or even intelligible in modern circumstances.

11. Giles, *Patterns of Ministry,* 36–38.

12. Ibid., 71–97, offers a good summary of the problems and some useful solutions.

Chapter 5

1. Even where the full classic pattern is maintained in terms of ordinations, it is sometimes only remotely connected with the functioning of the ordained. In few catholic communities is the diaconate truly a living order. The presbyterate is rarely a collegial body in anything more than name. The presbyter or priest, in fact, is often de facto bishop and deacon of the local church and may have little time and energy left for truly presbyteral work. Our primary concern here, though, is with the rites and networks of ordination itself and what they say sacramentally of our church life.

2. I base this statement on my earlier study of John, *The Mystical Way in the Fourth Gospel: Crossing Over Into God* (Philadelphia: Fortress Press, 1987), 104–8.

3. This was the usual Anglican position immediately after the Reformation; cf. Paul F. Bradshaw, "Ordinals," in *The Study of Anglicanism,* ed. Stephen Sykes and John Booty (London: SPCK; Philadelphia: Fortress Press, 1988), 151.

4. The outsider, of course, is in danger of misreading another's tradition. I mean the following example only as a tentative exploration.

5. *Augsburg Confession,* Art. XXVIII, read literally, appears to express a desire to retain the office of bishop if it could be done without compromising the gospel. Some, however, argue that this was only a rhetorical device to disarm the opposition.